EDINBURGH JUNE '96

To D[...]
He[...]

Love from

Fiona & Peter:

16/1/63.

Ramshackledom

Ramshackledom

A CRITICAL APPRAISEMENT
OF THE ESTABLISHMENT

by
L. G. PINE

LONDON
Secker & Warburg

First published in England 1962 by
Martin Secker & Warburg Limited
14 Carlisle Street, Soho Square, W.1

Printed in England by
The Windmill Press Ltd
Kingswood, Surrey

Contents

CHAPTER ONE

The Antique Country

BE they rebuilt a hundred times, the English law courts will always have something of drabness and musty gloom. Something of Dickensian description hangs about the various court rooms in the sham Gothic palace in the Strand. Little cause for surprise then that in the Lord Chief Justice's Court on that day in December 1954, the royal coat-of-arms which hung above the judge's seat should have antedated by six reigns the era of Her Majesty Queen Elizabeth II. The arms displayed were those of William IV, great-great-great-great uncle of our present Sovereign. They were brought to the Law Courts from Westminster Hall when the latter ceased to be the place of pleadings. They included the arms of Hanover, of which William IV had been King, but the sovereignty over which did not pass to Queen Victoria on her accession in 1837. This old coat-of-arms was, therefore, an emblem of part of British history; it depicted, for those skilled in heraldry, something of our history. It was an appropriate symbol for the scene which was to be enacted in that court.

An usher (the Cryer), came through the door behind the judicial dais and proclaimed the sitting of the Court. After this there entered two Registers, whose academic robes brought an unusual touch of colour into the sombre room. Then followed a splendid sight, six gallant Officers of Arms (the assessors of the Court), resplendently clad in scarlet tunics and dark blue trousers with golden stripes. They wore medals and decorations of honour, they carried cocked hats in their hands and swords were at their sides. They ranged themselves on either flank of the judge's seat. A few seconds more and there appeared the Lord Chief Justice of England, Lord Goddard. But not for him to vie on this occasion with his English judicial scarlet, against the colours of the assessor's uniforms. Lord Goddard was clad as a Doctor of Civil Law, in a light crimson gown and the doctor's black hat. Such colour as he possessed seemed little indeed beside the gloriously clad figure who sat with him. Sir Bernard Marmaduke Fitzalan-Howard, Duke of Norfolk and Knight of the Garter the Earl Marshal and Hereditary Marshal of England, was

7

clad as were his Officers, but with the added glory of the blue ribbon and star of the Garter. He had a magnificent plumed hat on his head. Lord Goddard bowed to him and doffed his cap as the Earl Marshal took his seat.

On this 21st December 1954, Lord Goddard was not in his usual Lord Chief Justice's Court. For this one day, the court room had become that of the Earl Marshal sitting in his Court of Chivalry. Lord Goddard was his Surrogate, empowered by the Earl Marshal to act in the present case. What was the case? One brought by the Manchester Corporation against the Manchester Palace of Varieties. The complaint? That the defendants had used the arms of the Corporation on the drop curtain of their theatre and (more serious) on the seals of their contracts and other documents. The result of the hearing was that the Court found for the Manchester Corporation, and the arms of the latter had to be given up by the Palace of Varieties. The Surrogate gave his carefully considered judgment in January 1955.

That is only the barest description of the happenings in the Court. By sitting and giving judgment the Court affirmed its own existence after an abeyance of 219 years. It had not sat since 1735. As I watched the proceedings I was conscious of how much history really means in England, however ignorant of it we may appear to be. On my left sat Gilbert Harding, one of the representatives as he might be called, of a post-war Establishment. What use he made of the scene I do not know, but my secretary brought in a note from the B.B.C. which asked me to broadcast that night about the Court of Chivalry. When I did so, I said that that day I had seen English history come alive; and that in only one other country in the world could an institution be revived after a suspended animation of two and a quarter centuries.*

It is, in fact, the case that only the Vatican State today can rival or perhaps surpass England as a country where the past can be brought back. Of course the Vatican State is more than a country. It is the centre of the largest and most highly organised religion in the world. Interdicts, sentences of deposition of kings, crusades,

* For a full account of the last sitting of the High Court of Chivalry see the book published by the Heraldry Society in 1955. This is: *A Verbatim report of the case in The High Court of Chivalry* of the Lord Mayor, Aldermen and Citizens of Manchester versus The Manchester Palace of Varieties Ltd. on Tuesday, 21 December 1954.

these are all weapons which have been laid away for some centuries. That they remain in the papal armoury ready for use when the time is ripe, need not be doubted; nor is it altogether hard to imagine circumstances in which they could be used again. Realistic in the ways of this world, the Papacy has not issued an interdict since Fr Paolo Sarpi rendered that launched against Venice in 1606 a fatuous fiasco.* But let a country once more hold a population of keen, believing Catholics (as the U.S.A. might one day) and then the government of that land must be wary should it differ from the Papacy.

The Papacy, as Lord Macaulay wrote, is the only modern institution (other than the Christian Church) which was contemporary with pagan Rome. It is something for a secular state to vie with so ancient an institution. Yet England has this antiquity. Our monarchy can soberly be traced with genealogical certitude to the fifth century; with reasonable probability to the third century, when Wodin or Odin was divinised in gratitude for his heroic qualities. Our system of nobility dates back to the aldermen of Anglo-Saxon times. Nobles we have always had, from our earliest annals. Earl is a title with a near millennium of life in England. The Established Church reckons its age as 1300 years, though there was a British long before there was an English Church. Witenagemots, National Assemblies, Parliaments, they are written into the parchments of our history; we have the first historical annals and in the Doomsday Book the first census, and even the first rude and painful Schedule A.

Small wonder then that in a land so full of history we should re-enact the past, and be influenced by it. One of the most dramatic of our stagings is that famous Mystery Play, the State Opening of Parliament. In the Middle Ages, those who were solicitous of the

---

* Leopold von Ranke in his *History of the Popes* (Bell, 1906), vol. II, page 122, described the interdict against Venice decreed by Pope Paul V. First the government of Venice were excommunicated. Very short periods were allowed for recantation, three of eight days and one of three days. Then, after the failure of this measure, all churches in Venetian territory were prohibited from performing divine service, i.e. they were laid under interdict. In reply the Venetian government called on the faithful clergy to carry on with the services. The result was that the clergy obeyed the state with the exception of the orders of the Jesuits, Theatines and Capuchins. As their members obeyed the Pope's command, they were forced to leave Venice never to return. The failure of the interdict is attributed to the teaching of Fr Sarpi who held that within its territories the state must be supreme.

welfare of the ignorant, put on plays in which the mysteries of religion could be made clear to them. No such conscious intention has inspired those who have surrounded with great pomp the Sovereign's opening of Parliament, yet the result is the same. In the wilderness of the twentieth century when mass ignorance is rendered more hideous because it pretends to knowledge, the Queen's opening of Parliament shows a picture of what Britain once was but is not now. The Queen proceeds with solemn pomp to her Palace of Westminster, using it at her pleasure as her own. Peers and Commons alike are her tenants. She takes her royal seat on the magnificent Throne in the Lords. From this splendid position she can see in the far distance the Speaker of the House of Commons, as he sits wearing the wig and gown of English legal officialdom in the Lower Assembly of Parliament. The Queen is surrounded by her family and the officials of her household, and these include the Earl Marshal and the thirteen Officers of her College of Arms. Her Majesty is magnificently attired and wears the Imperial Crown upon her head. Before her are ranged her Lords Spiritual and her Lords Temporal, the latter in their ceremonial robes of ermine and velvet. Everything in the scene conspires to exalt the position of the Sovereign. But something is wanting to complete the picture. Her Majesty sits in Council with her nobles, but where are the faithful Commons, the members of the Lower House? Clearly on this great occasion they must be called to hear the words of their royal mistress. An official messenger, Black Rod, is sent to summon them to the presence of their ruler.

Black Rod walks with dignified yet speedy tread towards the entrance of the House of Commons. When he is within a few feet of the door it is swiftly and unceremoniously thrust to in his face. Perforce he has to knock. A little wicket aperture is opened, and an official of the Commons asks him his business. Once it has been stated, he is allowed within the Chamber. At the bar of the Commons he delivers his message, and summons the Commons to hear Her Majesty's speech.

Then the Prime Minister, arm-in-arm with the Leader of the Opposition, and followed by the M.P.s, two by two, as in a school crocodile, troop obediently along the hall of the Palace of Westminster until they halt before the bar of the House of Lords. There they stand in a small space where hardly one tenth of the 630 M.P.s can be accommodated. In this humble position they listen to the Gracious Speech from their Sovereign. The scene in 1960 is exactly as it would have been in 1560, as far as the relative positions of the various parties of Parliament are concerned. A print of the Parliament of Queen Elizabeth I shows the enthroned Sovereign faced by her nobles and with her faithful Commons at the bar of the Lords. A picture of Elizabeth II opening Parliament would show the identical positions of Crown, Lords and Commons, the three constituents of Parliament.

This picture, however elaborate and splendid, is a sham, a charade or play-acted pretence. The Prime Minister who stands in the humble position at the bar, has written the Queen's Speech. He has given her advice which, unlike most advice, she must accept. For what if she did not? She would have the doubtful privilege of receiving the Premier's resignation; then of sending for the Leader of the Opposition who would refuse to accept office in a House where he had no majority. In the crisis of 1936 Edward VIII was advised that should the Baldwin government resign he would find it impossible to form a new one. The Lords themselves are very largely recruited from the Commons. Many of them owe their places to the Premier who stands so obsequiously behind them.

In the course of four centuries the balance of power has changed completely, so that the Commons are through their leader the dominant party in the Parliamentary triangle. All Bills from the Commons require, it is true, the assent of the Lords and, finally, of the Crown. The Lords may object, may amend, or even simply refuse to pass. Their actions are qualified by the fact that they cannot oppose in any way the passage into law of a measure which the Speaker of the rival House has certified to be a money bill. Also, even when the Lords do refuse to pass a Bill, they know that it will automatically become law if it is presented again in twelve months. As for the Royal assent, it is a very long time since it was withheld.

Then as to the ceremony of shutting the door of the Commons's Chamber in Black Rod's face, this is only a reminder of the famous event of 1640 when Charles I appeared in the Commons to arrest the Five Members. Since then no Sovereign has been allowed to enter the Commons, save when George VI obtained the Premier's permission to visit a newly-repaired Chamber. A brusque treatment must likewise be given to the emissary of the Crown as he walks towards the Commons.

So there we have, as it were in brief epitome, the solemn British re-enactment of past history. Although the English have little historical memory, unlike the Irish, Welsh and Scots, they are happy to steep themselves in their historical background. Often the traditions of England are quite recent affairs as traditions go, but they harden with great rapidity, and become in popular apprehension the bulwarks and memorials of a remote past.

How far can this be an advantage, and how far is it the sign of an outworn national consciousness? There is quite frequently an absurdity about our worship of the past which even the most sensitive patriot cannot deny. The membership of the House of Commons is 630. The original Chamber was burnt down in 1834 and rebuilt between 1840 and 1857. It was partially destroyed by Hitler's bombers and rebuilt after the war. Neither in 1857 nor in 1951 was there the slightest attempt to provide sufficient seats for all the 630 members. This was brought clearly to my mind when I visited within a matter of weeks the Parliament building in Helsinki and the Houses of Parliament at Westminster. In Helsinki, the Commons number 200 members. In their Chamber there are 199 seats. The guide then explains that in every Parliament they elect one member as Speaker. There is a special seat for him. It is all so rational and sensible. So, too, is the voting system of using coloured lights to indicate majorities. It makes one wonder why British M.P.s in a crowded House are so hard put to find space in which to sit.

As for the House of Lords, that is the main constituent of our system of nobility. Its peculiarities are so numerous as to make it the most awkward titled system in the world. Although peers and their connections form one of the never-failing standbys of the British press, not one Briton in a hundred knows what a peer is, despite the fact that the doings of our aristocracy are recorded almost daily in the newspaper.

I must not diverge from my course for I shall deal in full detail later with the peers. My purpose in this book is to describe our titled system from the *fons et origo*, the Crown itself, down to the last two entries in the Table of Precedence, the ranks of Esquires and Gentlemen. Yes, strange as it is, an Act 'for the Placing the Lords' (i.e. the Table of Precedence), which was passed in the reign of Henry VIII, is still the governing instrument in matters of precedence. It can easily be imagined how difficult it is to determine the position of some modern personages under the terms of this 400-year-old Act. In 1540 there was no Cardinal Archbishop of Westminster; so he is not found in the Table. A pretty problem for those who have to entertain him among their guests of honour. Where are they to place him? The absence of the Lord Mayor of London from the Table is much more puzzling as London had its Mayor long before 1540. The Prime Minister was unknown to official Precedence before 1905 when Edward VII settled the matter by Royal Warrant. On the other hand, the Precedence Table does afford some guidance to the position of someone like Mr Antony Armstrong-Jones, who, until he was created Earl of Snowdon, was entitled to a place in it as an Esquire.

The fact that the Precedence Act has had to be stretched this way and that to accommodate persons such as the High Commissioners of the Dominions is an indication of how overridden we are with all sorts of ancient customs. It is quite understandable that there has to be a method of placing persons by their rank.The utter inadequacy on official occasions of the present system can be demonstrated when it is realised that such an important minister as the Chancellor of the Exchequer ranks below the younger sons of earls, and far below the younger sons of marquesses. In other words, at a public function, Lord Valentine Thynne should come before the Rt. Hon. Selwyn Lloyd. The position of Lord High Chancellor is still what it was four centuries ago, when there was no first minister as such. Today the Chancellor, great and august head of the legal profession though he may be, is usually the Prime Minister's choice. In short this old Table of Precedence needs to be rewritten in accordance with the facts of modern life.

What is true of Precedence is true of the whole of the titled system. It represents something which once had relevance to the life of the current time but which now bears the same relation to up-to-date needs as the cuirass and helmet of the Household Cavalryman to his requirements in modern warfare. Most Englishmen with any feeling for the past like to see the Trooping the Colour. The uniforms of the cavalry and infantry recall glorious deeds in our imperial past. Now that we are to have a small professional army of less than 200,000, it might be a very good idea to put the whole force into scarlet for ceremonial occasions. Obviously the drab khaki and the hideous battle-dress would be used for practical work and for campaigning. I think a march once a year down Whitehall, of the peerage in ceremonial robes and coronets, like that in *Iolanthe*, would be an enormous draw; not only tourists but the natives themselves would be willing to pay to witness it. To expect a fully efficient and realistic

Upper House composed of the same materials is, by parallel, to expect our troops in the brilliance of scarlet and gold to soldier in the Aden Protectorate or the jungles of Guiana.

We cling to the past, we are developing a mania for old buildings and old things. Anyone who tries to move a 200-year-old cottage or barn is accused of vandalism, just as if he were trying to interfere with Winchester Cathedral. A barrow in Wiltshire, long ago ransacked for hidden treasure, probably by thieves who lived under the Heptarchy is levelled by a farmer. The ensuing outcry would lead one to suppose that he had bulldozed Stonehenge or tried to take over Salisbury Cathedral Close. Not everything handed down from the past is worthy of preservation. We tend to preserve and maintain everything over 100 years old. Yet we allow the huge Victorian houses to degenerate into foul tenements. We build new houses, on agricultural land, to rehouse people from the slums of the Industrial Revolution, but perfectly well-built houses, of five or more stories, have been allowed to degenerate into slums, for want of stringent laws to prevent their misuse.

To sum up, we are in danger of becoming an antique country. Our parallel state, the Vatican, and the Roman Catholic Church, remains ever the same and yet is perpetually changing. She distinguishes between the essential and the non-essential. Within the last few years evening Communion has been brought in in order that Catholics may not find the conditions of our material civilisation a barrier to the reception of the Sacrament. In other words a non-essential, the hour of the celebration of Mass, has been varied, but the essential, the Mass or Holy Communion remains.

By similar reasoning, we ought in Britain to be able to distinguish the important from the inessential, and so to reform our titled system on a common-sense basis in order to make it serviceable to our modern needs. In the meantime any truthful description of it must inevitably produce some ludicrous and humorous passages.

CHAPTER TWO

The Crown

WRITING early in the present century, Viscount Bryce remarked that a man of intellect and strength of character could yet produce a decisive influence on the British or the Spanish monarchy, in other words make it something beside a mere confirmatory stamp. The outcome of this prophecy in the case of the Spanish monarchy may be seen after the death or retirement of General Franco. Its failure in Britain can be read in the pathetic account of the Duke of Windsor, *A King's Story*. In this the ex-King Edward VIII laments how unequally matched is a constitutional sovereign in contest with his Prime Minister. Without in any way seeking to dwell on that unhappy episode in modern history, it can accurately be said that it marked the last chance for the re-emergence into any real power of the British Throne. Today the monarchy has only two direct powers left which can conceivably be exercised without the advice of politicians. One is the bestowal of the great Orders of Chivalry, the Garter and the Thistle.* the Order of Merit and the Royal Victorian Order. The Order of St Patrick is also technically reckoned among these, but this Order is now never bestowed, in consideration of the fact that twenty-six out of thirty-two Irish counties are outside the jurisdiction of the Crown. The second royal power is that of sending for one political leader in preference to another, as in the case of Mr Macmillan instead of Mr Butler after the resignation of Sir Anthony Eden. Even then how far is the choice exercised independently and without the advice of an outgoing Premier? Otherwise apart from these two exercises of prerogative, none of the other royal prerogatives can be used except on advice of the ministers. A wish from the Sovereign may be construed as a command, as when George VI desired the discontinuance

---

* The bestowal of The Garter and The Thistle lapsed from the power of the Sovereign from the era of George I till 1946 when Mr. Attlee as Premier in agreement with Mr. Churchill as Leader of the Opposition restored it as the personal gift of the Crown. Even so, it is understood that the Sovereign will inform the Premier beforehand of the proposed appointment. On this subject see *The Queen's Orders of Chivalry* by Sir Ivan de la Bere, 1961 (p. 73).

of the presence of the Home Secretary at the birth of the heirs to the throne, or when Her Majesty the Queen did not approve of public houses being called after Prince Charles. These are still, however, wishes, not orders, nor are they of first-class importance.

The monarchy has declined in power, even in indirect influence, very greatly since 1867, the date of publication of Walter Bagehot's classic, *The English Constitution*. To anyone reading this now, there is the same interest as attaches to a book like Scott's *Waverley*, a picture of times long past. We see in Bagehot's list of contents, words which have a familiar ring – the Cabinet, the Monarchy, the House of Lords, the House of Commons – but which have a different meaning today. Enormous changes in our Constitution have taken place within this century, and within less than the last fifty years. It was not until 1914 that a measure for permitting manhood suffrage found its place on the Statute Book, and it was only after half a generation had perished in the terrible holocaust of Flanders, that a vote for each male at twenty-one became effective. In 1919 came the vote for women of thirty. In 1929 womanhood suffrage followed. Within fifteen years the Government of Britain had been changed from an oligarchy with some 5,000,000 voters, to a full democracy. Along with this great change, came also an insistence on the role of the State as opposed to the individual. This attitude, expressed in movements as different as Communism, Socialism, paternal Conservatism, and Mosley's Blackshirtism, meant a huge extension of Government interference and control. The multiplication of the electorate instead of giving firmer democratic control has rendered governments immune from criticism, and without fear of their electors, provided that certain material benefits are kept going. Before the war, unemployment was the master fear which dominated politicians; since the war, full employment is the great object set before all the parties as the most important matter. Full employment with an ever-growing volume of cars, refrigerators, television sets, and washing machines – this is the consideration which is in the forefront of the minds of electors and, therefore, of the politicians. One is tempted to think of the *panem et circenses* of Ancient Rome. Absorbed in a material well-being never known before, as far as the mass of the people are concerned, the electors are uninterested in anything that does not directly touch themselves. Colonial development means nothing to them; foreign affairs mean very little, not even a pause in their round of selfish materialism; at the most they concede to the danger of war a tribute to fatalism, 'let us eat and drink for tomorrow we die'. Even the sufferings of the old-age pensioner often fail to stir the mass of the workers.

In a political atmosphere of this kind, all the old constitutional language has changed its significance. One has only to read the memoirs and lives of those former political giants, like Asquith or Lloyd George, or Churchill's account of his early life, to feel in another world. Over the last forty years we have become a full democracy, the first in the world. There was no real democracy in ancient Athens, for more than half the population were slaves. Even France after the French Revolution had votes only for men. But today we have in England a system in which the people are supreme, and the terror of the politicians but where the politicians can do as they like provided material well-being is kept up. It is rather like the Carthage of the Punic Wars; as long as trade is good, then the oligarchy can do as it likes. In England this has meant a constantly growing interference with the life of the ordinary citizen. The multiplication of laws knows no limit, although one of the most urgently required reforms in the country is a holiday from law-making, and a drastic overhaul of the existing laws.

Within this new atmosphere stands unchanged the ancient system of titles, stemming from the Crown, the Fountain of Honour. For the Crown is at the head of the titled system and its *raison d'être*. In theory, nobles occupy the same relationship to the Crown as planets around the central sun, or as the fixed stars were conceived to do in the days of Ptolemaic astronomy. The theory was expressed in these terms by Elizabeth I in talking to Sir Philip Sidney; nobles were set around the sovereign to enhance his or her glory to the mass of lesser folk. This conception is as outdated as the pre-Copernican scheme of the universe. From the majority of the nobles the modern Crown receives little support and from some of them actual injury. Nobility was once of service in leading men's views up to the highest dignity of all, the Crown. Today with three-guinea daily allowances, and with paupers among the aristocracy, the peerage is tarnished and discredited so that it takes away from the lustre of the monarchy itself.

I shall describe the modern peerage at length in its proper place, but for the moment I mention it as illustrating the isolated position of the Crown. The ancient sentiments of devotion to the sovereign and the archaic terms still applied to him or her, such as the Fountain

of Honour, have been emptied of all meaning. Yet at the same time
that monarchy has been deprived of all effective participation in the
life of the country, there has grown up a most unhealthy attitude
towards it. Its position has become very similar to the role which was
for so long assigned to the Mikados of Japan. No power, but a
species of divinity hedging round the monarch, and keeping the
vulgar herd at a distance (there is inevitably a reminder of Horace's
Ode, Liber III, Carmen I, *Odi profanum vulgus et arceo*).

Some of the conventions affecting the monarchy become ridiculous
in proportion as we know its history. One must not touch royalty, a
curious prohibition, when one considers the behaviour of the Tudors,
the Stuarts or George IV. Perhaps it came in with Queen Victoria.
It certainly was in with Edward VII, as one of his Jewish hosts found
when he put a steadying arm to the king.*

Then there is the practice of the non-royal party to a royal marriage
walking behind his partner, and with hands folded behind his back.
This practice was soon to be adopted by Princess Margaret's husband,
Mr Armstrong-Jones. Again in former days a sovereign was quite
capable of stopping and talking, even drinking with a subject. No
such thing can now occur, not even stopping the car for a couple of
minutes. One woman who asked this favour was told that the royal
car would graciously slow down as it passed her house. We are
constantly told that the sovereign and the rest of the Royal Family
now move easily among the people. In fact this is not true, for far
more protocol than ever before known now governs the movements
of royalty. Any child who reads historical accounts of Plantagenets,
Tudors and Stuarts, knows perfectly well that the sovereigns of
olden days, who had a great deal to say in the government of their
country, had also little inhibition in mingling with the people. The
possession of real power renders aloofness unnecessary. Conversely
the decline in power brings a defensive quality in its train.

I would be perfectly willing to agree that much of what appears
standoffishness and exclusiveness on the part of our royal house is
due to the ridiculous absorption with the minutiae of royal doings

---

* It was certainly not enforced however by the Duke of Windsor at least when
he was Prince of Wales. In his book, *A King's Story*, the Duke recounts (p. 140)
how he was drawn out of his saddle when in Canada. 'Lifted off the horse's back
by strong hands and passed like a football over the heads of the veterans. Dis-
hevelled, shaken and breathless, I eventually found myself on the platform
clutching the crumpled notes of my speech.'

displayed by the press. *De minimis non curat lex*, but this does not apply to journalists. If the Queen has a bruise on her leg, it is solemnly photographed and commented on as soon as observed. That she may take part in stalking and that this cannot be accomplished without knocks and cuts is simply ignored, and cannot be left to imagination. If the Queen and Prince Philip are photographed standing or sitting, their every gesture has to be interpreted. Prince Philip in one photograph of the Indian tour was seen looking at one of the pools at the Taj Mahal. We are told with high seriousness that he was looking at his reflection in the water. Sometimes the accounts verge on indecency as when we are told of lights going out in certain rooms, on the occasion of a royal honeymoon, but most of the newspaper descriptions tend to be just silly. Mr Armstrong-Jones takes a job, and there is a battery of photographers to meet him as he comes in, with relays of reporters to watch him throughout the day and tell us how long he took for lunch and whether he has sugar in his tea. The most trivial remark made by royalty is chronicled in the newspapers as though it were one of the greater sayings of some eminent ruler of the past.

What then is the real position of the Crown today? It stands virtually powerless as it presides over the liquidation of the former British Empire. Each year the area of royal (though purely nominal) jurisdiction grows narrower; each year the area which the Sovereign Lady can visit *qua* sovereign grows less. A tour of Pakistan and India is a melancholy revisiting, as Head of the Commonwealth, of places where her grandfather, uncle and father were Emperors. The Queen sits as a guest while a president occupies the throne or seat of state. In all the countries which are now independent republics, or on the verge of becoming so, there are numerous memorials to past British imperial rule; memorials which show the rapid descent of our world-wide power in the last forty years. India and Pakistan are republics with the poorest of allegiance to a symbol, the Head of the Commonwealth; Burma is not even within the Commonwealth but became a republic as it were overnight. Ghana and Ceylon, Nigeria and Singapore, all have gone or are going the same way as India and Pakistan. South Africa, set on the path to becoming a Boer-dominated Republic, has, in fact, left the Commonwealth while this book was being written. Thus another of the Queen's titles is wrenched away.

In short we are witnessing a dramatic reversal or retraction of the claims which have always been advanced for the English or British

Crown. From the days of Offa, King of Mercia, our sovereigns have always thought of themselves as imperial rulers.*

A valuable empire apart from the American colonies could be formed out of those territories which Britain voluntarily surrendered before 1914. They were as widely scattered as any seaborne empire could be, and included Dunkirk, Tangier, Minorca, Cuba, Manila, Corsica, Buenos Aires and Montevideo, Java and the Ionian Islands. This would have formed a large, rich and varied empire for any major power. Most of these territories were held by the British quite securely, owing to our command of the sea. If we add these possessions, plus the American colonies (having in mind the vast nation those colonies became), to the Empire as it was in 1922, we can say without too great hyperbole that half the world at one time or another has been under the British flag. Even in the war of 1939-45 our traditional policy of sea power made it possible for us to take over the Italian possessions in Africa. Libya and Italian Somaliland and Eritrea became territories in possession of His Majesty. Although a large part of our own empire was overrun by the Japanese, even this was recovered. When the Second World War ended we were still, at least nominally, the mightiest empire in the world's history.

How swift has been the descent from that greatness! We have moved far from the day when Winston Churchill, speaking in London at the Mansion House on 10th November 1942, said: 'I have not become His Majesty's first minister in order to preside over the liquidation of the British Empire.' Suffice to say that the proud title of Empress of India has been borne by only one Sovereign Lady (her present Majesty has never been Empress), and that the official style of the late King George VI had to be altered. Queen Elizabeth II is Head of the Commonwealth, an expression which is almost a matter of ceremony alone, without much meaning. With the present rate of change, the Queen will in a decade or so have under the royal writ only the United Kingdom. It may be said that the position must be accepted. We must learn to become as Sweden. But the comparison is not true. Certainly Sweden was once a great power, with possessions around the Baltic Sea. The frame of empire broke with Charles XII's death in 1718, and the Swedish colonies were gradually lopped away within the succeeding hundred years. The Swedish population has never exceeded the resources of the homeland. Clearly the huge numbers of people in overcrowded Britain are not

* For a fuller account of the rise of the imperial idea see Appendix I.

supported by our own production of food. We have reached our predominant position because we are the centre of a world-wide community. For over a thousand years our rulers, in direct descent from Egbert of Wessex (Her Majesty is his 63rd successor) have been overlords of some territory or other. This position cannot now be abandoned lightheartedly without the consequences being very serious. We have as it were a top-heavy crown coruscating with a brilliance to which the shrinking reality lends no support.

We are told that by our good sense and moderation we have done what no other imperial power has ever succeeded in doing, and have created a Commonwealth out of an old-fashioned imperialism. Quite. It will be observed that in a matter of sixteen years we have not only ceased to refer to the British Empire save in the historical sense; we no longer talk of the *British* Commonwealth. It is the Commonwealth pure and simple. The adjective 'British' must not be used. Ireland is a republic, so is Burma, and neither is a Commonwealth member. The republics within the Commonwealth can easily take a line contrary to that of Britain, as India did over Suez. It was said at one time that, whatever else might go, there would always be the Crown as the bond of the Commonwealth, but all the old constitutional bonds have snapped or are being loosened preparatory to being snapped.

So we are in the position that our Sovereign has an Imperial Crown without an Empire in which to wear it. Can anything be done about this situation? I believe the position is still capable of being redeemed. The history of England (I am not, for reasons which will appear, referring to Scotland) is a success story over many centuries. One dominion succeeds another. The empire in France was lost. Within a century and a quarter came the settlement in North America. When the Americans declared themselves independent, the future colonies of Australia and New Zealand were being explored, and Canada was at the beginning of her wonderful strength. But the old Empire of pre-1914 has now gone. What can take its place? There are no more habitable continents to be explored, but there are two important possibilities for Britain. One lies in the European Economic Community, with which we ought to link up. If we did I think we should become the predominant partner in a group which would then include over 200,000,000 persons. We are holding back for two declared reasons, the special position of our agriculture, and our Commonwealth economic preferences. I think that the real reason is that within the Community we should have to agree to a limitation of sovereignty. That limitation would, I think, be more apparent than real. In a community of seven nations, the United Kingdom would be industrially the most powerful, and far and away the most mature politically. It would be well worth the sacrifice of some freedom of action, in the tariff sphere of economic nationalism, to take the hegemony of the western European world. Our Sovereign would not be the monarchical head of United Europe, but the ancient crown of the only large European country to remain a monarchy would inevitably gain fresh lustre.

The other possibility for the revival of Britain is in participation in the space age which is at present dominated by the giants, the U.S.S.R. and the U.S.A. Vast progress has been made towards a landing on the moon, with untold possibilities beyond that. It is agreed among scientists and technologists that far-reaching commercial benefits will accrue to the nations which are leaders in the sphere of space exploration. Britain has so frequently been the leader in exploration and scientific discovery that her failure to participate in this latest venture is a measure of judgment as to her lack of adventurous spirit. The new Elizabethan age opened with the great British triumph in climbing Everest. Is this promise without fulfilment?

While I write these words, England has been full of admiring reports of the great success of the Queen in her tour of India and Pakistan. It was objected that Her Majesty's progress through the Indian peninsula recalled the old-time splendours to which her imperial predecessors were accustomed. There were the military parades, the maharajahs, the tiger shoots, the Taj Mahal, all the old princely India, and not enough of the realistic side of modern India. But as Head of the Commonwealth the Queen has fulfilled an impossible task. There is probably no other record in history of a monarchy which has held imperial power, the sovereign of which has toured the former province in the guise, as it were, of an interested friend. The personal triumph of the Queen's personality in India was astounding, never has she shown herself more regal. But here is no continuing city. George VI toured South Africa, but nothing has prevented the dismal march of events in that country. The same fate of separation could affect India likewise, with a change of government. When commands are no longer possible, then the only bonds are those of sentiment and loyalty. There is no longer a common union in allegiance to the Crown. Try how we will to disguise it, the Commonwealth, which is not even British, is a curious and eccentric development out of the former British Empire. I cannot see that it will endure, and if and when it goes, the imperial crown will then be supported only by Great Britain and the six counties of Northern Ireland, with possibly an island or barren rock scattered about the oceans, to recall what was once *Imperium Britannicum.*

Either, or better still both, of these contingencies, participation in Europe and in space ventures, would give back to our crown that imperial glow which belongs to it, almost as of right. Without it, the Crown is like a mighty headgear set upon a poor and ailing body, liable to topple over the wearer.

CHAPTER THREE

The Royal Family

A SINGLE, often completely unnoticed fact, of little significance in itself, reveals how closely the members of the Royal Family are linked with the reigning sovereign. In an ordinary non-royal family all members have the right to a certain share in the family's coat-of-arms. In the Royal Family, the members have no personal coat-of-arms until the head of the family, the sovereign, chooses to bestow it. Thus the Royal Family being *sui juris* is completely different from any other, and reasoning which would apply to e.g. a peerage family has no applicability to royalty. The reasons for this particular heraldic rule is that the royal arms of dominion, i.e. of the ruling authority in the state, cannot belong to anyone but the wielder of that authority, until he or she is willing to delegate the use of the royal insignia.

Furthermore, the Sovereign until elevation is a mere junior member of the royal house. All his or her importance is derived from office. Had the course of Edward VIII's life run normally, he would have married early in life and had children. In that case there would have been no George VI or Elizabeth II. The latter would have been Princess Elizabeth, a member of the Royal Family carrying out a useful function, assisting in various royal tasks, just as Princess Alexandra does. The Crown is in this sense everything, the individual nothing.

This fact explains why members of the Royal Family are never as other people, never free, always with the full glare of public scrutiny upon them. They are adjuncts to the Sovereign. Their task is to help the wearer of the Crown carry out his or her obligation. Once in a half-century the early death of an heir to the throne, or the childlessness of a sovereign, may bring a royal scion from the wings to the centre. So it was when George IV died, when the Duke of Clarence predeceased his father, Edward VII, and even more so when there occurred the abdication of Edward VIII. But for the most part, brothers, sisters, uncles, aunts, cousins, etc. of the reigning Sovereign take a very subsidiary position in the scheme of things. They are born to their round of duties and they must carry them out. No doubt this often goes against the grain, and they wish to kick over the bounds set for them by their birth. Hence there is the possibility of one failure to each generation, human nature being what it is.

At present the royal duties are shared between the Queen herself, the Duke of Edinburgh, Queen Elizabeth the Queen Mother, the Princess Margaret, the Duke and Duchess of Gloucester, Princess Marina, Duchess of Kent, the Duke and Duchess of Kent and the Princess Royal. Notably absent from the list are the Duke and Duchess of Windsor. It has been made abundantly clear that their position in the Royal Family resembles that of Christians in the world, in being in it but not of it. Ever since his abdication the Duke has been at least a fugitive, transient visitor to his native land, the news of his homecoming tucked away in a few lines in the more obscure column of a newspaper. It was expressly laid down that his Duchess should not have the style of H.R.H., a distinction the sole explanation of which is the undoubted fact that the Crown as the Fountain of Honour can make what rules it pleases with regard to titles.* The post the Duke received during the Second World War, after the fall of France, was the Governorship of the Bahamas, hardly a position of outstanding responsibility. It certainly seems at least curious that a man of the Duke's enormous experience should never have been offered anything of value since the Bahamas appointment. I have explained that royalty has not to be judged by the canons of ordinary folk, but among ordinary families the word 'spite' would probably be used in this connection.

As the degrees of nearness to the throne decline, the amount of responsibility declines also. The Earl of Harewood and his brother do not share in the royal duties and are much freer to follow their own wishes.

The round of royal tasks is truly formidable. At one time I was much concerned with a charity which I found was one of two hundred of which the Queen Mother was patroness. It cannot be assumed that the patronage of these numerous good causes involves nothing more than a perfunctory message through a second or third secretary. The royal patrons in these cases really do concern themselves with the subjects to which they have given the cover of their august names. How often there must be a simulation of interest, and how often this

* Here, by the way, is an example of a small but real exercise of power.

is completely justified, can be left to what must surely be the understanding imagination of the reader. There is no part of the national life untouched by some member of the Queen's family, and as there are not more than a dozen men and women to serve the work of a vast Commonwealth, it is little wonder that royalty are not noted for longevity.

For these reasons, the development of a young member of the Windsor family is watched by the older hands with great anxiety. I had the privilege of working for two years with Princess Marie Louise when she was compiling her highly successful memoirs. I have no intention of repeating the confidences which I was able to share with her but it is no breach of trust to say that the late Princess was more than once extremely concerned over the development and training of the royal scions. The way of a prince or princess was hard, Princess Marie Louise felt, and she knew how much sacrifice it had meant in her own case. She had spent nearly fifty years as a virtual widow, and had never attempted to remarry. She had acted in this self-denying and noble manner because she could not recognise the validity of divorce. Her German husband had divorced her, but she felt that marriage was for life. Consequently she could not think that a member of the modern generation could ever put self interest before the clear duty imposed upon royalty by the circumstances of birth. The abdication of Edward VIII in order to marry a woman who had already been married twice and whose ex-husband was still living, remained to the Princess a tragedy, and tragedy which was incomprehensible. In her attitude towards the crisis in Edward VIII's career, Princess Marie Louise held the same views as those which the ex-King ascribes in his memoirs to his mother and his sister – in his own words 'I became conscious of their growing consternation that I could even contemplate giving up the throne of my forbears'.

It can be understood without much effort of the imagination how greatly the royal family were alarmed at the recrudescence in a new generation of the same problem, divorce, which had produced such serious consequences in the time of Edward VIII. The rumoured romance of Princess Margaret and Group Captain Peter Townsend raised in a most acute form the dilemma before which Edward VIII succumbed. There is no need to prolong here and now the minute accounts which were circulated in all the most popular newspapers. Suffice to say that the Princess put principle and duty before inclination, and thus lived up to the ideals of the older generation.

How far is the popular press in England responsible for the creation of the very stories about royalty to which it gives such enormous publicity? Clearly the matter of the friendship between the Princess and Townsend could not have been a press creation, or there could never have been the serious discussions on the subject which took place between the Princess and Archbishop Fisher. But the public attention was unduly focused upon the romance, and in a most prurient and unhealthy manner. A much worse feature of the Princess's affairs as handled in the newspapers was the linking of her name with the names of successive young men who were described as eligible bachelors. One newspaper compiled a list of the twenty or so escorts of the Princess. On several occasions when it was thought that an engagement was likely, it happened that biographies of the potential bridegroom appeared in the press. It also followed as a general, though not invariable rule that the man in question married someone else shortly afterwards. In some newspaper offices there were proofs describing the engagement of Her Royal Highness with X or Y ready to be rushed out as soon as the news was official. I have one of these souvenir proofs. I have also met some of those young men who were put forward by the newspapers as prospective husbands.

Generally, as I have said, the treatment of the Royal Family, particularly Princess Margaret, in the British press has left much to be desired. Persistent snooping and constant silliness in the newspapers do no real service to its members. Quite apart from the fact that they are of little interest to most readers, it is merely ludicrous to have description and comments on the Royal Family's casual remarks and actions. When some important news really comes, it is often unforeseen and misunderstood. The engagement of Princess Margaret and Antony Armstrong-Jones is the prime case in point. When it was announced, no one in Fleet Street was ready. There was a frantic scurry for information. Fortunately for everyone concerned, the Armstrong-Jones family is of county rank, both the father and grandfather of Princess Margaret's husband having been High Sheriff of Caernarvonshire. The family was, therefore, found in *Burke's Landed Gentry* and in a few other less easily consulted reference works. But despite this, very little was known about Antony Armstrong-Jones.

One of the consequences of the press being caught unawares is that it is apt to take its revenge when once it has the news under control. A deluge of material about Armstrong-Jones began to fill the newspapers after their recovery from the first shock of surprise at the announcement. The latter occurred on 26th February 1960. The following day a typical 'popular' headline was that of the now defunct *News Chronicle*, 'Margaret Engaged': 'Her husband-to-be, a society photographer, is moving in to Buckingham Palace'. This same newspaper went on to say: 'On Monday Mr Armstrong-Jones, who is giving up his work as a photographer, moves into Buckingham Palace at the invitation of the Queen and Prince Philip, where he will be busy keeping in touch with arrangements for the wedding.'

However much blame may be attributed to the press for blowing up trivialities to an unjustified size, no newspaper can resist the legitimate query and accompanying comment. Why should Armstrong-Jones give up his job and become in effect unemployed? Why should he at once move in with his future in-laws? Again, within ten days there had been the birth of a second son (Prince Andrew) to the Queen and the deaths of Countess Mountbatten and of the Marquess of Carisbrooke. Family mourning was ordered for one week. Ordinarily the engagement would not have been announced until the end of the mourning period. The seeming haste of the announcement gave free rein to the press in its speculation regarding the future of the royal couple. Would Armstrong-Jones be made a peer? If so what would be his rank? That of an earl, a marquess or even a duke, for no one seemed willing to elevate 'the squire of low degree' to merely the lowest rank of the peerage, to be simply a baron. On this subject there was speculation right up to the eve of the wedding. In one instance a viscounty was named, with a small wayside halt in South Wales to provide the territorial designation. As the Armstrong-Jones family has its roots in North Wales, it would have seemed pointless to give a title derived from the south. It turned out, of course, that this guess had no more foundation than any of the others. As it happened Armstrong-Jones remained untitled until a few weeks before the birth of his child. What was the occasion for the ennoblement of Princess Margaret's husband? He shows no sign of following a public career, such as that of colonial administrator. Few, indeed, would suggest such a thing. The problem of finding something for him to do, since apparently he could not continue in his chosen occupation, was partly solved by giving him an unpaid post with the Council of Industrial Design. One result of this was certainly to bestow an unprecedented press coverage on the Council's offices in the Haymarket on 23rd January 1961, the date when the appointment was taken up. Considerable attention was given in the press to the important question: does Mr Armstrong-Jones take sugar in his tea? But did this post demand a title? Since then the problem of work for the Earl of Snowdon has now been solved by his appointment as artistic adviser or art director to the *Sunday Times*, which at the same time went into the field of colour magazines. There was a great deal of criticism of this appointment, on the ground that it would draw the Royal Family, if only in the popular imagination, into some form of participation in business and even in politics, since the *Sunday Times* has a definite Conservative bias. The criticism of the appointment cannot be dismissed as jealousy on the part of rivals in the newspaper industry. Large numbers of ordinary people who have no connection with the press are appalled at the thought of a royal, or even semi-royal, participation, even by implication, in the affairs of a newspaper. The hard fact remains that this question can be asked: would Lord Snowdon have been offered the post with Thomson newspapers had he not married Princess Margaret? If not, then his appointment is a recognition of the advantage of a famous name, allied so close with the Crown.*

To revert to the matter of the title, its absence does have an embarrassing effect in social matters where precedence and rank are of importance. In the great majority of cases a woman derives her rank from her husband. (A Queen regnant is an exception, so too is a peeress in her own right.) But in the case of Princess Margaret the Princess has retained her rank. This was not the case with Lady Patricia Ramsey, who before her marriage in 1919 to the Hon. (later Sir) Alexander Ramsey relinquished her style of Royal Highness and the title of Princess. Lady Patricia, who was the younger daughter of the Duke of Connaught, was then granted the style of a Duke's daughter and precedence immediately before Marchionesses of England. Similar arrangements were made when Princess Katherine of Greece married Major Brandram. She renounced the style and title of H.R.H. and Princess – this course of action lay in her own power, she being of the Greek royal house and not within the jurisdiction of the British Crown. When, however, by marrying a British subject Lady Katherine came under British law, she was granted by the Crown the rank and style of a duke's daughter.

* See Appendix V.

The Fountain of Honour can decide how its waters shall flow. Rules can be made and unmade – remember the denial of the style of H.R.H. to the Duchess of Windsor. Still it seems curious that after her marriage some arrangement similar to the Ramsey and Brandram cases was not adopted for Princess Margaret. Had she been permitted to renounce her royal rank and become Lady Margaret Armstrong-Jones, the ensuing situation would have corresponded to the numerous marriages of dukes' and marquesses' daughters with plain misters.

On the practical side, the marriage will – at least one hopes – put a final term to the hateful bandying about of the Princess's name over the past ten years. The attitude of the press towards Princess Margaret seems to have been summed up in the slogan which one London street newsvendor kept on his board: 'Princess Margaret–sensation.'

Yet despite everything which can be said about the vulgarities and offensive behaviour of the press, despite all the denunciations to the Press Council, and all the tears shed by those whose feelings have been outraged by articles which come close to the truth – the fact remains that the British press in giving minute attention to the royal house recognises that the Crown and the Royal Family belong to the nation. The nation has the right and the wish to know what is happening to its own treasured possession. Let anyone cast his or her mind back to the times when releases from the Palace have been slow. At once a great volume of inquiry has flooded in from readers to the newspapers, which are then impelled to act. There is in fact genuine interest taken by the British in their Royal Family. The danger is, however, that by reporting every little item, e.g. every turn in Prince Charles' convalescence after appendicitis, interest can be converted into indifference or even dislike.

Then, too, the presence of souvenirs of royalty all over the country in the form of pictures and photographs is another indication of interest, for unlike the pictures in continental countries of political leaders, our royalty has no pressure group working on its behalf.

The ownership of our royalty by the country means in effect that a stricter code exists for royalty than for anyone else. In common parlance they 'have to watch their step'.

The circumstances of the abdication of Edward VIII might well have proved fatal to the continuance of the Throne. It is not so much a question of divorce, as the possibility of a member of the royal house preferring his or her own inclinations to the path of duty.

Without doubt it is a very hard lesson to learn, but the dedication to the service of the Empire and Commonwealth made by Princess Elizabeth in South Africa during her parents' tour of that country, is expressive of the spirit in which every member of the royal house must approach his or her task.

The sense of dedication is not something which can be conveniently left to the occupant of the Throne. The true supports of the Crown today are not the nobility in any sense, but the members of the Royal Family who are bound up with the temporary head of that family, the reigning Sovereign, in his or her task. That is why, as regards the Royal Family, there simply cannot be the facile attitude 'why shouldn't he or she do as they like', which is prevalent in the England of today. If one of our royalty takes such an attitude the whole position of the monarchy is threatened.

I would sum up the position of the scions of the royal house by saying that the future of the monarchy could be seriously compromised by the behaviour of someone who is unlikely ever to become sovereign. A junior member's conduct could reflect upon the whole conception of monarchy in this country. The Royal Family is thus united, either in stability or in failure. I do not propose to embark upon any discussion of the utility or otherwise of royalty to our country. I hope that the facts which I have given in Appendix One will demonstrate sufficiently that monarchy is an institution so ancient in this realm that it antedates even the unification of England into a nation from a set of warring tribes; that this majestic sequence of sixty-three sovereigns over more than 1,100 years from Egbert of Wessex to Elizabeth II has only once been interrupted for the brief space of eleven years; and, finally, that the repudiation by the British people of this republican experiment was so strong as to enable them, for the sake of the monarchical principle, to endure the succession of bigots, foreigners, fools and rakes between James II and George IV. There is a deep underlying consciousness that monarchy and nationality go together. An England without a monarchy would be a miserable, snuffling republic, without glamour and almost without history. What is not so generally understood is that this realm of England has always been an empire, and that without greatness it cannot continue. If, therefore, it is destined to become an American satellite, there will be no place in it for a monarchy.

It is often said that the Crown and the Royal Family cost the country so much, which would be saved without them. Putting on one side any consideration of the cost of a republican regime, some simple facts cannot be too often reiterated about the real position. The nation makes a very good thing out of the Crown lands. It is only necessary to refer to so easily accessible an authority as *Whitaker's Almanack*, to learn that the Crown lands were made over to the nation by George III in 1760 in return for a fixed allowance. At the time of the surrender the gross revenues amounted to some £89,000 and the net return to about £11,000. If we take a typical recent year (1952-53) we find that the total receipts by the Commissioners of Crown lands amounted to over £2½ million. Out of this nearly £1 million surplus revenue was paid to the National Exchequer. It is instructive to set against this vast profit the figures of the Civil List which gives the allowances paid to the Queen and other members of the Royal Family. In the same period the Queen received £475,000 which was broken down as follows:

	£
Her Majesty's Privy Purse	60,000
Salaries of the Household	185,000
Expenses of the Household	121,800
Royal Bounty, alms and special services	13,200
Supplementary Provision	95,000

In addition, five other members of the family receive the following sums:	
Queen Elizabeth the Queen Mother	70,000
The Duke of Edinburgh	40,000
The Duke of Gloucester	35,000
The Princess Margaret	6,000
The Princess Royal	6,000
To this should be added £9,000, being provision made for Princess Margaret on her marriage	9,000

	166,000
	475,000
	£641,000

It is a simple fact that the nation has benefited enormously from the bargain struck 200 years ago. It is a compact renewed at the beginning of each reign, but it is possible for a new sovereign to revoke the arrangement and take back the management of the Crown lands. The country would not then have to find the £700,000 required at present for the upkeep of the Royal Family. Equally, it would not receive the near-million profit; so on balance the bargain would be one of great loss to the Exchequer.

The Crown lands often have a pedigree from a remote period. When William I had his Doomsday Book compiled, he noticed many properties which were of ancient demesne, i.e. which had been Crown property for a long period under the Saxon kings. Thus Crown properties go back in many cases to the beginnings of the English settlement in the fifth century A.D.

When we turn to another consideration, the name and descent of our royal line, we find that the main stem is Germanic. It is only indirectly and through the female line that we can connect the Windsors with the Stuarts, Tudors, Plantagenets, Norman and Saxon kings. The main stock of the royal ancestry is that of the Hanoverians, the Electors of Hanover. This family is known as the House of Guelph, and its origins can be traced back to the period in the late fifth century when the Roman Empire came to an end in the west. The name originates as that of one of the Germanic leaders whose kingdoms were founded on the ruins of the Empire. The family were settled in Bavaria, then in Italy, where they were Marquesses of Este at the end of the eleventh century. In 1235 the head of the German line, known as Otho the Child was created by the German Emperor, Duke of Brunswick and Lüneburg. In the sixteenth century the Dukes of Brunswick were the heads of the family, while it was from the junior line, the Dukes of Lüneburg, that the first Elector, Ernest Augustus descended. He was made Elector of Hanover in 1692, and it was his son George Lewis, who became George I of England in 1714. George I was the great-grandson of James I, and succeeded to the throne on the death of Queen Anne, because all the other descendants of James I were Roman Catholics. It was thus a curious accident which brought this Hanoverian prince to the throne of Britain. Of the first four Georges little good can be said. Apart from all else they are uninspiring figures in our history. It was only with Queen Victoria that respectability became the distinguishing mark of the Royal Family. It has often been pointed out that the upbringing of the future Edward VII was too severe, and this has been attributed to the influence of the Prince Consort. But the Queen knew that between the young Prince and 'my wicked uncles' there was only her own life. That she had a sound instinct would be agreed by most students of the life of Edward VII. Respectability came again with the Queen's grandson, George V, and has continued.

It is not easy to see in what way there can be excessive or any other kind of pride in this ancestry. True our great-grandparents did not have the same feelings about Germany as we have perforce been compelled to entertain. Twice within a lifetime to have the peace and prosperity of our country shattered by the same nation, is to feel distrust and dislike of that nation. Especially when in the last struggle, elements of the most horrible bestiality were revealed, such as the avowed purpose of exterminating the Jews.

What is the name of the Royal Family? The older school history books of fifty years ago referred to the House of Hanover; occasionally a book of the Victorian period referred to the House of Guelph. I once saw a heading above the name of Edward VII: House of Saxe-Coburg-Gotha. It is well known that this king disliked this description of his line. The subject of the designation or surname of the Royal Family did not become active until the First World War. Then, with the King's near relatives at the head of the nation's German enemies, it became necessary to try to clear up the dynastic background of our royal house. Various authorities were asked for the royal surname. Sir Bernard Burke had long before given it as his view that so ancient a royal line, *atavis edita regibus*, could not possess a surname as having been illustrious before surnames became common currency. His son, Sir Henry Farnham Burke, then Garter King of Arms, took much the same view. If there were a surname it was Guelph. The Gordian knot of the difficulty was cut by George V assuming for himself and his family the name of Windsor. In 1917 he issued a Proclamation to the effect that 'We out of our Royal Will and Authority, do hereby declare and announce that as from the date of this Our Royal Proclamation Our House and Family shall be styled and known as the House and Family of Windsor, and that all the descendants in the male line of Our said Grandmother Queen Victoria who are subjects of these Realms, other than female descendants who may marry, or may have married shall bear the said name of Windsor.'

The only alteration of this has been in 1960 when the Queen stated that in certain cases of fairly remote descendants, they would bear the name of Mountbatten before that of Windsor – the introduction of a hyphenated name into our Royal Family for the first time, though this practice is common enough in the continental monarchies (c.f Prince Philip's family name.)

Despite this introduction of the typical Montmorency Robinson or Plantagenet Jones surname into the Royal Family, the name of Windsor has been adhered to. After her accession to the Throne, the Queen announced that her family name and that of her children would continue to be Windsor.* The subsequent proclamation of 1960 did nothing to alter this.

Still the Englishness of our Royal Family is rather artificial like the deliberate assumption of the name of Windsor. Basically the Sovereign's house is Germanic. It was to sever the Germanic ties that the Proclamation of 1917 was made, and at the same time all Germanic titles were discontinued. No human being can do anything about his or her birth, nor ought it to be held against anyone. That does not, however, mean that anyone should be proud of German ancestry.

The German nation is at present working its passage back to civilised sanity. While the progress is yet continuing, it seems peculiar that the Chief Magistrate (the eighteenth-century term for the Sovereign) of the allies who overthrew Germany, should refer to her German ancestors. One wonders at the amazing contradictions of royal etiquette. The Queen's Gracious Speech from the Throne is written for her; on other official occasions the speeches follow a set pattern and are as harmless as the sentiments of a *deus ex machina* in a Greek play. Why then did the Queen make what many English people would regard as the *faux pas* of referring to what is best forgotten, the German origin of the House of Windsor? Again, on another occasion there was a reference in a speech by the Queen to the Tudor tyranny of her great predecessor, Elizabeth I. Surely the unseen monitor could have done something about this hardly tactful utterance regarding one of the greatest of English sovereigns.

To sum up the royal position: Britain's monarchy, as I have said, is of her essence. It is an accompaniment of greatness, and woe to us if we do not build for a future of greatness. We cannot become dwellers in a glorified Main Street. We are great or nothing. With the monarchy goes the Royal Family. The members are the main support of the Crown today. They share in its work, and must uphold its

---

* An interesting work on this subject is *A General History of the House of Guelph or Royal Family of Great Britain* by Andrew Halliday. For the Queen's Proclamation of 1960 and the history of Prince Philip's family, see Appendix II.

standards. They simply cannot evade their responsibilities. Hard it may be but true that the princes and princesses are their country's property. They must live up to a high and exacting task, to assist the Queen in her many duties. The press has a vast preoccupation with regal matters. It pushes this to extreme limits, but it does reflect a certain public interest and even more important it reports what has actually happened to royalty. It behoves royalty, then, to be very well advised. Little real blame can attach to a newspaper which tries intelligently to prepare for what it thinks is a coming event. But it does suggest how great is the circumspection which must govern the lives of royalty whose least action is likely to be misinterpreted.

CHAPTER FOUR

The Fountain of Honour and the System of Titles

THE Sovereign is the *fons et origo* of the titles held by British subjects, a matter which is expressed by saying that the Queen is the Fountain of Honour. Just as the ceremonial of the State opening of Parliament recalls the events of history, as in a living mystery play, so the whole of the titles system is to be seen as the necessary connection and extension of monarchy. Royalty has always hitherto been accompanied by nobility. The theory has been that the nobles of the land were supports of the Crown; in another sense they were mediators between the Crown and the people. To bring out this point properly we need only look at the Coronation ceremonial. After the monarch is crowned, the peers of the realm come forward to do homage to her. The homage ceremony is purely medieval. "The Peers of the Realm, who are then in their seats, shall kneel down, put off their Coronets, and do their Homage, the Dukes first by themselves, and so the Marquesses, the Earls, the Viscounts and the Barons, severally in their places, the first of each Order kneeling before Her Majesty, and the others of his Order who are near Her Majesty also kneeling in their places, and all of his Order saying after him:

"I, N. Duke or Earl, etc. of N. do become your liege man of life and limb and of earthly worship; and faith and truth I will bear unto you, to live and die, against all manner of folks. So help me God.'"

Everything connected with the system of nobility and title is of a very antiquated nature, reaching back to the days when the sovereign really ruled the country. The fact that this ancient system is still with us is due to the extreme conservatism of the British, which has sought to retain the old nobility and titular machine while attempting to modernise it.

In reality what has happened is that despite all the efforts of reactionaries, diehards and unbending conservatives, the titled system has been so greatly altered that it might not unreasonably be said to be in process of extinction. This is true despite the undoubtedly large increase in titles in the present century.

The peers cannot any longer, with a few honourable exceptions, be considered as supports of the Throne. No one who reads the popular press (or the less popular for that matter) over a few months could seriously imagine that this bevy of noble lords who make, or sometimes even write such good journalistic copy are helping the Queen in her task. Married very frequently, as frequently in and out of the divorce courts, engaged in all sorts of curious escapades, sometimes behaving very foolishly, at others downright badly, the limelight lords are not the stuff which props a crown.

Leaving for the present their moral or immoral qualities, and looking at the system itself we can see its steady disintegration. No non-royal dukedom has been created since 1874, when the Grosvenor family received the dukedom of Westminster. In 1900 the dukedom of Fife was created at the time when the Earl Fife (he succeeded his father in that title) was married to Princess Louise, the eldest daughter of King Edward VII. But his dukedom must really be reckoned as royal just as much as that of Edinburgh. It is true that the creation of so great a dignity as a dukedom was never a frequent event. Even if we included Fife, there are only five cases still extant in the British peerage which have been created in the nineteenth century. There are Wellington (1814), Sutherland (1833), Abercorn (1868), Westminster (1874) and Fife (1900). Yet making every allowance for the rarity of the appearance of a new dukedom, one within eighty-seven years is a low record in the peerage annals in the last 200 years.

It would seem that ducal honours are no longer created save for royal personages or those who marry royalty. Both Marlborough and Wellington received dukedoms; the certainly not inferior services of Sir Winston Churchill would probably have been rewarded with an earldom had he wished for a hereditary title.

Turning to the next honour in the peerage, that of marquess, it is a quarter of a century since the last marquessate, that of Willingdon, was created. Previously this title was a more frequent honour than that of duke, there being on the roll of peers thirty-nine marquesses to twenty-six dukes (excluding all royal dukes plus Fife). Here again then we have a wasting honour. The waters from the Fountain do not course through these higher channels of aristocracy.

What of the earls? There are over 200 of them and their creation is still a fairly commonplace matter in certain circles; a retiring Prime Minister may expect reasonably enough to be given an earldom. Likewise a distinguished soldier or sailor, as in the cases of Wavell,

Alexander and Mountbatten. By contrast the number of viscounts is much smaller, being less than 140. With baronies, which are the common or garden form of peerage, we reach the really large numbers, closer 600 than 500. Yet even with these very numerous peerages there is an enormous difference between the position now and as it was even thirty years ago. Very few peers are able to live on unearned income. Most have to eke out their private means by work of some sort or another. As a consequence, the order of peers has greatly declined. It is very hard to keep up a high idea of the dignity of a person with whom one is working every day.

There was a time when every peer was rich, just as there was a time some 300–400 years ago when to be a peer was synonymous with membership of the Privy Council. The idea that riches and titles go together dies very hard in any mind which is not that of a peer or a peer's near relation. There are many people throughout England, and, indeed, throughout the world, who cherish the legend of their family's claim to a title. Merely to be noble is sufficient reward for the majority of them, for whom indeed it is a case of *noblesse oblige*. But there are a large number of inquirers and seekers after peerage honours who are out for more solid rewards than the gilding of a coronet. Are there estates to go with the title? is the question which they put forward. The idea still exists that titles and estates go together. Indeed, until comparatively recent times they did, for a bestowal of land usually accompanied a grant of a title. One need only refer to the cases of Nelson, Wellington and Marlborough where an estate went with the peerage title. This has now ceased to be the practice; the last instance occurred after the 1918 war when money grants were made to such great leaders as Earl Haig.

Then again most people know vaguely that landed property and money sometimes go unclaimed and are held by legal authority until an heir appears. Some may even know that the funds in these cases are held in Chancery, and their ideas of that Court are derived from Dickens's novel, *Bleak House*. It must be a great blow to these eager aspirants to learn that the total amount held in what is now the Chancery Division of the High Court does not equal one-tenth of one of the huge fortunes which people think to be hidden beneath the late Victorian Gothic in the Strand. Not even the Golden City of Manao could have satisfied all those who feel that millions lie waiting to be claimed with a dormant barony or earldom. The Supreme Court Pay Office in the Law Courts is a place of disillusion-

ment. About £1½ million is held untraced or unclaimed, and most of
it is in small sums, spread over a multitude of beneficiaries. So prevalent is the mental juxtaposition of wealth with nobility, that the
Pay Office have thought it worthwhile to issue a leaflet on the non-
existence of the Drake and other millions. In fact, the British aristocracy has generally become somewhat impoverished, many peers
are downright hard up, while a few are so impecunious as to be a
menace to anyone who meets them.

However, at this stage I am only concerned to point out how an
old conception (wealth as a necessary concomitant of lordship) can
survive in popular belief long after it has ceased to correspond to any
reality. In a more recondite manner the use of the phraseology Right
Honourable, as applied to peers below the rank of marquess is
another survival. It was originally used for Privy Councillors, and
as most Privy Councillors were peers, and nearly all peers were
P.C.s, the term Rt. Hon. came to apply to all peers. Comparatively
few of them are now members of the Privy Council, and yet by usage all
barons, viscounts and earls are addressed as though they were.

In this way bits and pieces of the old feudal, medieval scheme of
dignities linger on, while others drop out. The movement is nearly
always in one direction, that of a steady reduction in the ancient
structure. Sometimes, however, there is a revival. This occurred
with the order of baronets. There is something very peculiar about
this order which now consists of over 1,500 persons. A sure instinct
has made literary men choose their villains from among the baronets
far more than from the peers, although when a staid, respectable,
nameless, wealthy figure is required, a baronet is also often forthcoming. The order was cradled in the financial worries of James I's
reign. It would never have existed but for the Stuarts' perennial need
for money. It was founded in order to pay for the colonisation of
Ulster, and so may be said to have created the modern Irish problem,
the division of Ireland into North and South. A further creation of
baronets took place under Charles I to finance the settlement of
Nova Scotia. With such beginnings, it is not surprising that the order
has experienced many ups and downs. Various privileges have been
lost, such as that of the right of the eldest son of a baronet to be
knighted at the age of twenty-one. This must have caused some pretty
confusions, especially when father and son had the same Christian
name. This particular privilege disappeared in the early part of the
last century, when the order itself became obscured; the presence of

its members at great functions such as a coronation was uncertain, and owing to the difficulty of checking without a proper record, impostors could pass themselves off fairly easily.

Ultimately, in the reign of Edward VII, the equivalent of a guild or trade union was formed to look after the interests of baronets. This was the Standing Council of the Baronetage, and a Register was also set up, in the care of the Home Office to keep a roll of baronets. *

When the Labour Party obtained full power in 1945, they set themselves against the creation of more baronets. Between the years 1946 and 1951 only six were created, all being the immediate-past Lord Mayors of London. In the ten years since the Socialists left office, some sixty new baronetcies have been created. The reopening of this honour was due to Sir Winston Churchill, but it has been maintained by his successors. If hereditary honours are to go on existing, there is much to be said for the baronetcy. Its possession does not give its holder a place in the House of Lords, nor does it prevent him from sitting in the Commons if he can get himself elected to a seat there. Equally, an inheritor of a baronetcy has no difficulty in not using the title if he does not want to, and there are no tiresome consequences. The same considerations apply to baronets as to peers; no estate or fortune is necessarily entailed with the title. For some reason which I cannot entirely work out, more baronetcies than peerages are inherited by cousins. In many instances there are holders of all sorts of curious jobs.

Had the precedent set by the Socialists been followed, it would have taken about four centuries for the order of baronets to disappear into extinction. Between 1611, when the order was instituted, and 1838, when Sir Bernard Burke wrote a book on the subject, 1,000 patents of baronetcies have expired. Working on a similar figure, I think the present list without fresh creations would last until the twenty-fifth century A.D.

What of the orders of knighthood? There are twelve great Orders of Chivalry in the following order of precedence: The Garter, the Thistle, St Patrick, the Bath, the Order of Merit, the Star of India, St Michael and St George, the Indian Empire, the Crown of India, the Royal Victorian Order, the British Empire, the Companions of Honour. Two of the above, the Order of Merit and that of the Com-

---

* On the Order of Baronets, the reader should borrow (it is long out of print) *The Baronetage under Twenty Seven Sovereigns*, 1308-1910, by an anonymous scholar.

panions of Honour confer no title, but the recipient is one of a small select band distinguished by the letters O.M. or C.H. after his name. Of the ten Orders which confer the title of Sir, four are practically in desuetude. In the case of the Order of St Patrick, the last creation occurred in 1934 when the Duke of Gloucester was made a K.P. In March 1961 the 9th Earl of Shaftesbury died. He was the last non-royal Knight of this Order, which now numbers only the Duke of Gloucester and the Duke of Windsor in its chivalry. Clearly there has been no intention of keeping up this Order since the twenty-six counties of Southern Ireland became the Irish Free State, or Eire, and eventually proclaimed themselves the Republic of Ireland. The banners of the Knights are still preserved and shown with reverential care in Dublin, but they are now really antiques. The Order is finished in all but name. Yet despite the separation of Southern Ireland from the British Commonwealth there has been no dearth of Irish servants to the Crown, particularly in the armed forces. The generals who hail from Ulster alone would have formed a brilliant chapter of St Patrick's Order, but most of them have been gathered into the conclave of the Garter.*

At this point perhaps I may interject two other Irish losses in the semi-feudal structure of the British titled hierarchy. The Officers of the Order of St Patrick were the Ulster King of Arms and the Cork Herald. The latter no longer exists. As we shall see in a later chapter, the Office of Ulster is united with that of Norroy King of Arms in the English College of Heralds. In the room of Ulster in Dublin Castle sits the Chief Herald of Ireland, an official appointed by the Irish Republican Government. In the various titled directories, *Burke*, *Debrett*, *Kelly*, you may search fruitlessly for the old picturesque heraldic trappings of the third kingdom. Irish genealogy and heraldry, while being ably pursued, share the nationalist direction given to their country's fortunes in other spheres of culture.

The Earl of Kilmorey who died on 11th January 1961 was the last of the Irish representative peers in the House of Lords. When Great Britain and Ireland were united by the Act of Union in 1800–1801, to form the United Kingdom, it was provided that the Irish peers should elect twenty-eight of their number to sit as their represen-

* I notice that Brig. Sir Ivan de la Bere, for fifteen years secretary of the Central Chancery of the Orders of Knighthood, makes much the same remark in his recent book, but adds that the Government of the Irish Republic would have strongly objected.

tatives in the House of Lords at Westminster. These peers sat for life, and were thus entitled to receive writs of summons to every Parliament. The mode of summons of the Irish peers was laid down in an Act scheduled under the Act of Union. To the Lord Chancellor of Ireland belonged the duty of issuing the writs for the election of the peers. With the establishment of the Free State in 1921 and the consequent abolition of the office of Lord Chancellor of Ireland, no machinery for the election of Irish peers existed. Hence there were no more Irish representative peers beyond those who were elected before 1921, and gradually this number dwindled away.

Elaborate arrangements had also been made under the Act of Union for the maintenance of the Irish peerage at 100. The new Republic did not care for titles of nobility, but it would have been quite easy to keep up the Irish peerage and to devise fresh machinery for its elections, had the will to do so continued.

All use of three of the remaining Orders of Chivalry – The Star of India, The Indian Empire and the Crown of India – has ceased, and they are rapidly on the way to the chivalric knacker yard. No Orders can survive the Empire they have been created to adorn.

Below these distinguished Orders of Chivalry which have now such an equivocal fate, lies the great common or garden order of Knighthood, which is technically known as that of the Knights Bachelor. Some forty or fifty of these knighthoods come along each Honours List. They are bestowed for varying degrees of public service. Judges of the High Court are knighted; Lord Mayors of London are knighted on taking office (and baroneted on laying it down). Provosts in Scotland are knighted. On the other hand almost all classes of society and occupation are to be found in the goodly company of Knights Bachelor. A jockey and a cricketer are knights but so far a professional footballer has not reached a distinction higher than C.B.E. There is a strong tendency to depreciate these ordinary knighthoods as coming far below the great chivalric orders. Yet it is from the order of Knights Bachelor that all the other orders have been derived. They have been hived off from it, for originally there could have been only the one basic order. Just as our public schools derive from charitable monastic foundations with aims very different from those of their distantly descended modern representatives, so the Knights Bachelor, who are often tradesmen, civil servants and municipal employees, represent the medieval knightly order. Most people I suppose have heard or read of King Arthur and his Round Table. When knighthood was in flower, in the early Middle Ages,it was a highly honourable calling and those who entered upon it received a consecration almost equal in solemnity to the ordination of a priest. It was because the general order was so exalted that particular orders were founded, to give an extra social lustre to it. In this way came the Garter in 1348. Edward III wished to emulate the Round Table of Arthur. He therefore chose the bravest and best of his knights, to form the new order. Of all the existing orders, the Garter preserves most closely its original character. Entry into it is very unlikely for anyone who is not of military rank and has not shown courage in action against his country's enemies.

The Order of the Bath shows very clearly how the special orders have grown from one original form. Many people have wondered at the date, 1399, for the foundation of the Bath. How could a king who had just dethroned his cousin and whose hold on the Crown was as uncertain as Henry IV's, have stopped at the beginning of his reign to found an order of chivalry? In fact, at each Coronation a number of aspirants to chivalry were knighted. The custom was for these gentlemen to have a bath before they received the accolade. The ascription of the foundation to Henry IV merely denotes that from the time of his coronation the selected knights were set more apart from their fellows. The last occasion on which a chosen band were bathed and knighted was at the coronation of Charles II. From that time on the order came to be given as a great honour, not limited to the occasion of a coronation.*

While we consider the gradual desuetude of much of the honours system, we must not forget that even in its attenuated application it is confined to the United Kingdom. The Governments of Canada, Australia and New Zealand have made it clear that they do not wish their nationals to accept titled honours from the British sovereign. A companionship in an order, such as the C.B.E., is the most that the Dominion citizen can expect (Canada does not now even submit a

---

* It should be added that perhaps all aspirants to knighthood underwent a ceremonial bath before being dubbed as symbolical of their putting off imperfections and moral slurs; but the Order of the Bath appears to have arisen from special dubbings of fairly large numbers at a Coronation, so that the name of the Bath became attached to those knighted on these occasions. It must be said that none of the learned writers on knighthood from the seventeenth century to the present have succeeded in overcoming the difficulties caused by lack of medieval records on the subject. Hence the Bath, like all the older orders, has an obscure history.

list of any honours other than those for gallantry). There are still a few titled persons in Canada or Australia but these are older people, whose titles were bestowed before the present ruling obtained. Needless to say, the same attitude to titles was taken by South Africa before its departure from the Commonwealth and by the coloured dominions or territories like India, Ceylon and Pakistan. This is a further restriction on the scope of titled honours.

It is when we turn to the House of Lords that we find, without any effort in seeking, continual evidence of a bolstering up and plastering over in the ancient edifice. In this light, the preamble to the Parliament Bill of 1910 (which when passed into law in 1911 reduced the power of veto of the Lords to a period of two years) contains some curious reading:

'Whereas it is intended to substitute for the House of Lords as it at present exists, a Second Chamber constituted on a popular instead of hereditary basis, but such a substitution cannot immediately be brought into operation' etc.* In the half-century which has passed since this was written, no step has been taken to substitute an effective Senate, Upper House or Second Chamber for the House of Lords. Several quite far-reaching changes have been made. None of them have been strictly logical but all have left loopholes for the preservation in some form of the outdated. Thus women have been given seats in the Lords. The judgment in 1922 of the then Lord Chancellor, the 1st Earl of Birkenhead, in the Rhondda case is still allowed to stand, as far as hereditary peeresses are concerned. Yet although a *sine qua non* in the reading of peerage students, this judgment does not dispose of the question. Why should a peeress in her own right not sit in the Lords (especially since life peeresses are now allowed to)?

To make the position regarding women peers completely illogical there is one case, that of Lady Ravensdale, where the same person has both an hereditary and a life peerage. The former is simply inoperative as concerning membership of the Lords, and she sits in the House solely in virtue of a life peerage conferred under the Life Peerages Act of 1958.

Similarly with the pay of peers, which is three guineas per day of attendance in the Lords. The agreement in 1957 to pay allowances

* The text of the Parliament Act 1911 can be seen in *The Future of the House of Lords*, a symposium edited by Sydney D. Bailey and published by the Hansard Society, 1954.

to peers is a belated recognition of the fact that peers are no longer of necessity wealthy men. But the smallness of the allowance does not arise merely from parsimony; at the back of it lingers the feeling that a nobleman ought to have financial resources of his own. This is precisely in line with the uninformed public's conception of large properties lying waiting to be claimed from Chancery in connection with dormant titles.

Another important feature of the House of Lords has been the introduction, at the same time as that of payment, of a system of leave of absence for peers. This operates successfully in that occasional attendance in the Lords is now much less likely. Peers can seek leave of absence at the beginning of a session. This being granted bars their attendance while the period of leave is in operation.

Feminine presences in the Lords and payments, however exiguous, for peers; these do not exhaust the changes of the last decade. In 1958 was passed the Life Peerages Act, which was intended, so it was stated at the time, to increase the democratic element in the Lords. Under this Act, Her Majesty is graciously empowered to use the prerogatives which are inherent in her sovereign position, and is allowed to create life peers, both men and women. The circumstances of life peerages are worth more than a cursory consideration for they are the *reductio ad absurdum* of the modern peerage and titled system. There can be no reasonable doubt that life peerages were created in former times. In the *Complete Peerage* (vol. VIII pages 751–753) twenty-nine instances are collected of peerages granted for life. The array of legal authorities who support the validity of life peerages is impressive, including the names of Coke, Selden, Comyns and Blackstone. Cruise in his work on *Dignities*, and the Redesdale Committee in their Report on Peerage Dignity, likewise agree that life peerages can be created. Sir Edward Coke in his *Institutes* (I.16.b.) says expressly that the sovereign may create either men or women to be noble for life. The last instance quoted in the *Complete Peerage* is dated 1758. Yet within a century of this in 1856 the House of Lords refused to accept the validity of a grant of life peerage to Sir James Parke, an eminent judge whose presence was felt to be necessary in the Upper House because of the congestion of legal business. He had been given a life peerage as Baron Wensleydale. The grant was challenged on the ground that no life peerage had been granted for 400 years, and that the power of the Crown to create such peerages, even if it had ever existed, had been lost by desuetude. The Committee of Privileges reported that neither the letters patent of life peerage nor the letters patent with the writ of summons annexed could entitle the grantee to sit and vote in Parliament. In order to resolve the difficulty created by the Lords in their perverseness, an hereditary peerage was conferred on Wensleydale.

The problem of legal congestion in the highest court in the United Kingdom continued. The Judicature Acts of 1876, 1887 and later, which merged the two systems of English law – Common Law and Equity – empowered the Crown to appoint a limited number of Lords of Appeal in Ordinary for the purpose of aiding the House of Lords in the hearing and determination of appeals, these peerages to be for life only, though undistinguishable in style from hereditary lordships.

Thus jealously guarded, the precious privilege of making a few judges (there are usually about a dozen in the House) into life peers has never allowed the Crown to save an elderly childless candidate for nobility from being rendered ridiculous. How absurd, and how cruel it is to make out letters patent in the following terms to someone who has always been childless or whose children are dead: 'to have and to hold unto him and the heirs male of his body lawfully begotten and to be begotten . . . he and his heirs male aforesaid', and so on.

The Act of 1958, therefore, came in to put matters right, to redress the balance between hereditary and life peers, and to turn the Lords into a more democratic body. Such was the announced intention, but it has been singularly stultified. In the first place, alongside the creation of life peers has continued that of the more 'respectable' type. There is no prospect whatever of the life peerages, as at present granted, overtaking the numbers of the hereditary. There are 924 peers all told, on the *Roll of the Lords Spiritual and Temporal* (published by H.M.S.O. periodically for 2s.). It must, however, be noted that Scottish peers who have no seat in the House of Lords are not included. In fact the number of peers exceeds 1,000. Of these only about forty are life peers. Out of the total number of peers, only about one-ninth or one-tenth really assist in the business of the House. Had the Life Peerage Act been worked in the spirit of its alleged intention, within five or six years the life peers who attended the House would have been equal in numbers with the hereditary peers who took a similar interest. But owing to the continued creation of hereditary peerages, and to the bestowal of life peerages very often on aged or infirm people, no appreciable alteration has taken place. Two very strange phenomena have occurred in connection with the life peerages. When a list of such honours is announced, it is often apart in time from the New Year's or Birthday Honours List. It is for all the world as though there were something of an inferior caste about these nobles for life, a gone-off nobility. Yet, by contrast, it is laid down in the instruments which govern their creation that their wives and children shall have the styles now accorded to the wives and children of hereditary peers of the same degree. This is really amazing, for it means that a son of a life peer may, if he chooses, be known, quite rightly, as the Hon. John X, though he is not and never will be the heir to a peerage.

Throughout most of its history the House of Lords has shown itself thoroughly eclectic; yet at times and in certain circumstances, as with iife peers, entry has been rendered difficult. Exit, however, except for treason, has been practically impossible. This doctrine has an extremely ludicrous aspect. The best commentary is to be found in the case of Mr Wedgwood Benn, with which I deal later on.

This historical position regarding surrender of peerages is perfectly clear. Such surrenders did take place right up to 300 years ago. In 1678 the House of Lords passed a resolution that (in the words of an earlier resolution, 1640) 'no person that hath any honour in him, and a peer of this realm, can grant or extinguish his honour but that it descends unto his descendants, neither by surrender, grant, fine, nor any other conveyance to the King'.

This resolution was upheld and the law reformulated in the Earldom of Norfolk case in 1912, when it was stated: 'There is no doubt that a man cannot alien a title of honour either by surrender to the Crown or by grant to a subject.'

In order to get things really complicated, these declarations were held to show the law, not only as it was in 1912 or 1678 but as it had always been. In other words, when in 1302 Roger Bigod surrendered his Earldom of Norfolk and Earl Marshalship to the King, neither the King nor the Lord Chancellor, both of whom accepted the surrender, knew the law. The surrender and acceptance thereof was invalid. Why could not the gentlemen concerned have waited until they could have learned some law? (See my articles on the Peerage in History and Law in the *Law Times*, 6 and 13 October 1960.)

This refusal to recognise the facts in the two instances of life peerage and surrender of peerages; this round declaration that the law is such, in clear contradiction of the historical facts, is not the only conflict between history and legal thinking in peerage law. The law, as it had been declared since 1678, is considered to have been the law always in the past, back to the furthest limit of legal memory, the accession of Richard I, in 1189. In addition the modern theory of peerage has been taken as the true construction of medieval baronial dignities. A writ of summons in the fourteenth century called to Westminster a person who was to counsel the sovereign. This man so summoned was one of the great feudal tenants holding *in capite* from the Crown. The theory of peerage law is that such a summons made of the person summoned a peer in the modern sense. This is the peerage known as a barony created by writ of summons, to distinguish it from a peerage created by letters patent. Over the past 500 years almost all peerages have been made by the latter method. There are surviving a few old baronies which are held to have been created by writ. In the case of these latter, they usually pass through the female as well as the male line. They are inheritable by females. Nothing more alien to the conception of a modern peerage can occur; in the few cases where a peerage created in modern times can be inherited by a daughter in default of a son, it is always in some special circumstances. The death of an only son on the battle-field before his father's elevation to the peerage (as with Earl Roberts' only son who was killed at Colenso in the Boer War); or the lack of male issue of a distinguished admiral, like Earl Mountbatten – these are the factors which help to insert a special remainder in the letters patent.

But the circumstances of the medieval 'peerages' are completely different. Our peerage, which in a form recognisable to us begins with the accession of the Tudors, arises out of the dignities of the old feudal system. In that system, title and dignity were never divorced from responsibility and land tenure. Peerage by the tenure was a reality, of which the sometimes quoted myth that whoso owns Arundel Castle is Earl of Arundel, is a reminder. The inheritance by a woman in the Middle Ages of a barony was in keeping with the feudal system, not with modern peerage law. The heiress carried her barony to her husband who thus obtained the title (if we stick to the modern phraseology). The very term 'baron' has come only after a long period of development to denote the lowest rank in our system of peerage. 'Baron' meant the King's man, the great tenant *par excellence* in the sense in which we refer to the barons who forced John to grant

Magna Carta, or to the Last of the Barons, who was incidentally, four times an earl.

Barony or peerage created by writ is simply one of those left-overs from the past with which the modern English State is struggling. In the judgment of 1922 to which I referred above, Lord Birkenhead was merely stating a fact when he said that it had never been intended to create women peers to sit in the Lords. It was, however, also a fact that under the Plantagenets, the modern legal view of peerage had hardly begun to crystallise. Consequently, to refuse *pace* the Sex Disqualification Act 1919, and its logical results, to admit the peeresses in their own right, was to argue back to an earlier stage in the evolution of peerage.

The anomalies and absurdities which I have exemplified are by no means exhaustive. The categories of the Scottish and Irish peers offer other entertaining conundrums to those in search of riddles and brain teasers as an alternative to *The Times* crossword. When England and Scotland became one country as Great Britain in 1707, it was laid down in the Treaty of Union that sixteen Scottish peers were to be elected by the body of Scottish peers, to represent that order in the House of Lords, such representatives to last for five years. A Scottish peer not so elected was not eligible to be a candidate for the House of Commons. Much more favourable conditions were granted to the Irish peers at the Union in 1800 of Great Britain and Ireland. They were to elect twenty-eight of their number to sit for life in the Lords. Those not so elected were eligible to stand for the Commons. Moreover it was agreed that the Irish peerage should be maintained at a strength of 100. If I were a fervent Scottish nationalist I think I should seize on the favouritism shown to the Irish as another wrong inflicted upon Scotland. The Scottish peerage declines steadily in numbers until it is possible to foresee the time when the electors and the representatives will be identical. Meanwhile, some Scottish peers are disfranchised. Irish peers have gained the best of both worlds, until at least the last generation. One of them, Earl Winterton, was M.P. for Horsham for forty-seven years, became Father of the House of Commons and on retirement was given a barony of the United Kingdom to enable him to continue in 'another place' at Westminster. He was indeed promoted two degrees downward in the peerage to become Baron Turnour; but to complete the air of Alice in Wonderland which now attends the Lords, he is referred to in the Upper House as the noble earl.

Today, no representative Irish peer sits in the Lords. None has been summoned to do so for forty years or more; no Irish peerages have been created in that period. The Irish peerage could become the delight of all who wish to be peerage fakers, of all who seek honours to which they are not entitled. For as an Irish peerage falls into abeyance or becomes dormant, what agency exists to check a claimant, or who would be interested in doing so?

Here then is a picture of the Upper House,* which clearly emerges as that of a medieval institution which has been altered here and there to make it less conspicuously ancient. Just as the State Opening of Parliament is a re-enactment each session of a state of affairs long past, so in all to do with the peers, there is a retention of phraseology long out of date. A peerage is created, the new peer must choose his title. He should, in fact must, consult Garter King of Arms, at the College of Arms, for it is by centuries-old custom the prerogative of Garter King to advise new peers on their titles. The normal procedure in the past was for a peer to take as a title something other than his surname. This practice has been badly broken and there are numerous cases in which the surname is taken, even the most peculiar of all forms of aristocratic nomenclature, a hyphenated name. However, traditionalism has triumphed to this extent, that every new peer must have a territorial formula to follow his new name, e.g. Lord Crooke of Carshalton, co. Surrey. The only instance which I know where this style has not been followed was in the title of Earl Attlee. Even then, the territorial designation was used for the Earl's second title: Viscount Prestwood of Walthamstow, co. Essex. The design is to keep up the fiction that we are living in the days when to be a lord meant to have physical ownership of an area.

Glimpses of the old-style phraseology occur in all sorts of documents. The Queen writes to

'Our Right Trusty and Well-beloved Counsellor Hartley, Baron Shawcross, one of Our Counsel learned in the Law;

Our Trusty and Well-beloved Sir Graham Cunningham, Knight Commander of Our Most Excellent Order of the British Empire;

Robert Browning, Esquire, Commander of Our Most Excellent Order of the British Empire;

William Brian Reddaway, Esquire;

William James Percival Webber, Esquire, Greeting.'

This is the preamble to the appointment of the above five persons to

* For the functions of the House of Lords as a court of law see Appendix III.

form the Royal Commission on the Press 1961. It would be the same for the appointment of any other Commission. Then each year one can read in the newspapers a list of new sheriffs headed with these words: 'The Queen, at a Privy Council at Buckingham Palace yesterday, *pricked* the rolls of Sheriffs for England and Wales for. . . .' Theoretically the pricking resembles the choice of a horse on a list. I once met a man who expected that year to be chosen High Sheriff of his county. He did not secure the appointment for another year, so perhaps the regal pin does move like the hand of blind Fate.

There is the old framework surviving from a remote past. Does it survive for any useful purpose? Can we stretch the skin farther? Will it break? Does it matter?

These are the inevitable questions which are prompted by a serious consideration of the System of Titles as it finds expression through the House of Lords. Clearly here is a medieval institution which by some miracle has survived long after nearly all the other bodies which were contemporary with it have disappeared. The characters of *Piers Plowman* or the *Canterbury Tales* would have been mightily astonished by the modern world, but some things would convey a meaning to them and one of them would be the House of Lords. It is a very remarkable thing that a House of Lords should still be with us and still retain any part in legislature. Search where we will in the devil's mess that was once Christian Europe, we shall find no other country with a similar institution still functioning. It is a marvel that it still does work. If I have highlighted the anomalies and absurdities, it is because they are there. They exist. They cry to be noticed. Even as I am preparing this book, a crisis has occurred in the peerage which makes even the creaking anachronisms that I have so far chronicled seem commonplace by comparison.

This event is the Wedgwood Benn or Stansgate case, in which Anthony Wedgwood Benn was debarred by law, when his father died, from renouncing the peerage he had inherited. I shall refer to this in detail in a later chapter.

For the present let me recount my own experience arising out of the Benn incident. I was asked by the Oxford Union to speak at one of their debates. The subject was: That the House of Lords must go. The original form of this motion had been to the effect that the case of Wedgwood Benn showed up the absurdity of our hereditary system and that the House, etc. I was asked to speak against the motion, and in the sequel my side won by a single vote, which is I believe the lowest majority since 1830 when, a certain Mr Gladstone being Secretary, the Union by one vote condemned the government of the Duke of Wellington. As I listened to the youthful speakers for the other side I noticed that the great majority of them believed in the need for a Second Chamber, though not for the House of Lords. I felt that had I taken the line that a reformed House of Lords should not contain any hereditary peers, I should have won hands down. It was the hereditary element which excited opposition. I realise that the radicalism of twenty is the incipient conservatism of thirty; yet I feel that there is a deeper opposition to the hereditary principle than can be conveniently explained by the impetuosity of youth.

Heredity is the crux, the *caput* of the whole matter. A House of Lords without hereditary peers is no House of Lords. In fact, if a scheme were to go through for life peers alone, I would regard it as an ill-named bad joke. If a reformed House is to be minus heredity, then it had better be called a Second Chamber, a Senate, or a Legislative Council. It will have nothing lordly about it.

Let us have the motives of those who seek the abolition of the hereditary peers completely naked and unashamed. Grant that it be done, then Majesty stands alone, the last sad relic of an aged system. The next move in the game is the abolition of the monarchy, or at the best its declination into something resembling the *fin-de-siècle* royalty whom Peter Simple likes to satirise when he writes of King Norman the Good. Once the rot has set in, it has to go on. Get rid of the hereditary peers and soon the hereditary sovereign will follow them into exiled penury. Which (to borrow Charles Kingsley's predilection for an opening pronoun) is exactly what most Left-Wing reformers want.

To sum up, thus far we have traced an ancient monarchy, a Royal Family, and a system of hereditary honours, crystallised in a House of nobles, with an elaborate hierarchy of chivalric orders. That monarchy is heavy with the weight of its immense and glorious past, so heavy that it might fall, through the very burden of it. The royal relations are there to steady and uphold the monarchy. On the whole they do so, but they cannot afford one weakening per generation. When the press goes too far in handling royalty, it should be recalled that it could not go at all without something to proceed on.

Then the Lords. They were meant for a support to the throne. It is easy to observe that strict morality has never been one of the aristocratic virtues. In the National Portrait Gallery there is the

anonymous portrait of an English nobleman of the reign of Henry
VIII (died 1547). With bulbous eyes, cruel visage, brutal in appearance,
coarse in manner, this nameless nobleman of 400 years ago looks at
us with undisguised dislike. One can imagine him 'drunk as a lord',
perhaps the person for whom the phrase was first coined. In each
generation one could draw from the records of the time a very un-
flattering account of the British nobility, written for the most part
by persons of their own social quality. The Italian historian, who
frequented the court of Henry VIII, Polydore Vergil, referred to
houses where *nec vir fortis nec femina casta*. Jonathan Swift echoed
the sentiment for the nobles of the early eighteenth century whom
he knew so well. Beckford, the disappointed would-be patrician and
author of *Vathek*, in his *Liber Veritatis* poured out a scorn the worse
because deserved. With all this contemporary evidence of depravity,
how could the aristocracy ever have been a support to the Crown?
Because in the past they had, with all their vices, some virtues and
splendida vitia, ill qualities of such strength that even foes must have
recognised their worth. It was for instance the patricians who decided
to fight Napoleon to a finish.

Today the morals of the aristocracy are probably better than they
have been in the past 400 years. It is the strength of character which
has so often vanished.

Titles are only the topmost poppies in the garden of aristocracy.
We must go on to deal with the numerous families of aristocratic
lineage, but without titles. First, however, the mountain peaks of
title must be cleared. What of the lords spiritual?

CHAPTER FIVE

The Lords Spiritual

IN the House of Lords there are twenty-six lords spiritual; the two Archbishops, of Canterbury and York, the Bishops of London, Winchester and Durham, and twenty-one of the remaining diocesan Bishops of the Church of England in England (but excluding any holders of Anglican episcopal sees in Wales, Scotland or Ireland). The holders of the five great sees which I have enumerated always have seats in the Lords; but the other twenty-one episcopal lords take turns at representation. Thus Birmingham may be represented by its bishop in one or more Parliaments, but his death or retirement can move the see down the list to await its turn once more. The movements among the diocesan bishops to take a seat in the Lords have something in common with the ding-dong battles of football clubs for places in the 1st or 2nd division.

How did the bishops come to be in the Lords in the first place? As the Parliament, like the Law Courts, grew out of the royal Court and the Great Council, it was natural for the magnates of the realm who formed the Council to form also the House of Lords. The Saxon Witenagemot had a history of 300-400 years before it became the Great Council of the Norman kings. Certainly the bishops were members of the Witan and the Council. They were so because they held considerable estates from the Crown. They controlled large areas of country and were able to bring vassals to the service of the state. They were, in short, among the great tenants of the Crown, and it was for this reason that they were present in the Assemblies which met to advise the sovereign. It might, indeed, be argued that initially the presence of these leaders of religion was due not to their stature as religious leaders but to the importance of their holdings as property-owners. But as against this view it is true that, save for their importance as pastors of the religious life of the country, the bishops would never have received the secular endowments which made them tenants of the Crown. Moreover, in the Council they spoke with a different interpretation from that of the lords temporal; they brought another viewpoint upon the problems of the age.

From the beginnings of English Christianity, the Church and State were closely connected. The Church was always established. Even in the great changes of the Reformation, an essential continuity of relationship was maintained. The Church before the Reformation was nominally under the rule of the Pope, like the rest of the Western Church. In fact there were many occasions when the English King was at variance with the Pope, and when the English Church supported its sovereign. Statutes of Praemunire were passed to prohibit appeals to Rome. Henry VIII's daring act in proclaiming himself Head of the Church of England would have been envied by many of his predecessors. He was enabled to carry through this revolution partly because of the growing anti-papal and Protestant feeling of the time.

The English Church is, next to the monarchy, the oldest institution in England, older by 300 years than the English national State. In no case has there been greater conservatism than in the retention of the various links between Church and State. The quarrels over the investiture of bishops which go back to the days of the Norman kings are reflected in the homage for the temporalities of his see which a bishop renders to the Queen. In the appointment of bishops the State has the controlling power. For many centuries the choice would actually have been made by the sovereign, but now it is exercised by the sovereign's chief adviser, the Prime Minister, who is said to be guided by the advice of the archbishops, and who has the invaluable services of the Patronage Secretary (the Prime Minister's Secretary for appointments). Just how the principal ecclesiastical appointments are made remains a profound mystery. The career of the late Bishop Barnes, once of Birmingham, caused immense controversies in the Church. So, for perhaps rather different reasons, does the presence of the Dean of Canterbury, Dean Hewlett Johnson. How were these appointments made? Did the Archbishop of Canterbury of the day recommend them? Then what of the late Dean of St Paul's, Dean Inge, so famous under the sobriquet of the Gloomy Dean? Some of his utterances and writings would have been in character with any agnostic outlook on Christianity. What too of the present Bishop of Southwark, who once sat as a Labour member on Bristol City Council? His appointment came about during the rule of Mr Macmillan. Was it felt that he would bring an air of unconventionality into the higher episcopal circles?

These are, of course, only flashes of the unusual among the mass of episcopal appointments and preferments which occur. Generally it is felt that safe men, mediocrities who can be relied upon, should be appointed to high office. So apart from the gleams of eccentricity just mentioned, most Church appointments can be depended upon to be secure. There will never be another Thomas à Becket, or an Anselm. It was an astonishing miracle that Temple was made Archbishop of Canterbury. There has certainly not been any successor to him in his prophetic work. I have a feeling that the powers of the established order were not sorry when he died. Then they could carry out the procedure outlined by Sir John Seeley in *Ecce Homo*, when he said that the conventionalists will resist a reformer as long as they can. When they realise that they must submit and accept the prophet's message, their next care is to embalm and stultify it. This is what happened with Temple's work. It is enshrined and nothing done about it. His successor, Archbishop Fisher, was a schoolmaster, first, last and always. When he was in an approving mood, he conveyed the impression that he was unbending with one of his senior prefects; archiepiscopal displeasure made the recipient feel that he was 'up' before the Head. There was perhaps too little that conveyed the air of a pastor. In fact, as has been publicly stated on many occasions, the archbishop's forte was administration. He improved the Church's administration. This could however have been done equally well by a small committee of sound business men – indeed, this is very much the work done by the Ecclesiastical Commissioners. But Christ's command was to preach the Gospel to every creature, and not to build up an organisation rivalling that of the State.

The ecclesiastical branch of the House of Lords has known many changes. In the Middle Ages there were many mitred abbots and priors who were entitled to sit in the Lords with the archbishops and bishops. Indeed, their claims to be present were considerable and came from the great area of landed property which they controlled. The majority of them did not sit in the Lords, but in the Convocations of the clergy, which they preferred. Still in 1529 in the reign of Henry VIII, the spiritual lords numbered forty-eight (of whom twenty were episcopal, the rest abbots of the greater monastic foundations). This compares with forty-four lords temporal. In 1539 the numbers were respectively forty and fifty. This was the first time in the history of the Lords that temporal outnumbered spiritual peers. The change was due to the dissolution of the monasteries which caused the disappearance of the abbots. Before that event took place nearly one-quarter of England was held by the religious houses, and this despite the statutes of mortmain passed by the medieval kings.

After the dissolution of the monasteries a small portion of the confiscated property was used to endow six new bishoprics. Of these one, Westminster, ceased to exist in the next reign, that of Henry's son, Edward VI. A vast jobbery and profiteering went on in connection with the confiscated monastic lands. Grasping courtiers, ever ready to catch the ear of majesty at its weakest moment, succeeded in filching from the royal exchequer huge areas and profitable investments. This was the origin of the greatness of the families of the Russells (Dukes of Bedford), the Cavendishes (Dukes of Devonshire) and the Cecils (Marquesses of Salisbury and Marquesses of Exeter).

It was nearly three centuries before there was an increase in the episcopal element in the Lords. This came about through the Union of Great Britain and Ireland in 1800–1801. At that time the Church of Ireland, the Protestant Episcopal Church, which was in communion with the Church of England, was by law established. The bishops of the Irish Church had, therefore, to be considered for inclusion in the House of Lords when arrangements were made for the Irish peers to be represented at Westminster. Under the fourth article of the Act of Union, four Irish lords spiritual were to sit and vote in the House of Lords of the United Kingdom. They were: one of the four archbishops of Ireland and three of the eighteen bishops, sitting in each session of the United Parliament, by rotation of sees. The Archbishop of Armagh, Primate of all Ireland, sat in the first session followed by the Archbishop of Tuam in the fourth. The rotation of the bishops was arranged in the same manner, and was to proceed perpetually from session to session.

The new spiritual reinforcements lasted barely seventy years. In 1869 the Irish Church Act disestablished the Church of Ireland. This Act was the work of a devout High Churchman, Mr Gladstone. The Act provided that after the end of the year 1870 no archbishop or bishop of the Church of Ireland should as such be summoned or qualified to sit in the House of Lords.

Thus the spiritual lords form today a small minority in the Upper House. Incidentally, it can be stated that they claimed originally to sit by virtue of the feudal baronies attached to their sees. In 1835 the Ecclesiastical Commissioners were incorporated and between 1835 and 1860 it was arranged that the lands of each bishopric should pass to the Commissioners. They administered them and paid salaries to the bishops out of the proceeds. It would appear from this arrangement that the claim on behalf of the spiritual lords to be fully peers of the realm collapsed with the placing in commission of the temporalities on which the claim was based. On any consideration it is a curious peerage which endures only during tenure of office. A bishop on retirement ceases to be a lord spiritual. From a fairly high place on the Roll of Precedence above the barons (hereditary peers) he sinks to no place, beyond the esquires of whom Mr Antony Armstrong-Jones was an example. Perhaps it has been this fate which has restrained the great majority of the 100 Archbishops of Canterbury from retiring. Most have died in office. Martyrdom has rather gone out of fashion, the last instance being that of Laud in 1645, so that our archbishops have tended to die at the advanced age to which a pure clerical life conducts them. The last three archbishops have, however, retired and all have been rewarded. Davidson and Lang each received a hereditary temporal barony, and as neither of these prelates had children, the peerage expired. Archbishop Fisher has made history by becoming the first retired Archbishop of Canterbury to receive a life peerage. Incidentally, he is also the first occupant of St Augustine's chair to be a Mason.*

This digresssion apart, I return to the presence of these ecclesiastics in the Lords. It can be justified only for the valuable witness which they bear to religion. We observe them rebuking sin in high places, criticising the faults of the secular state with its growing materialism, leading prominent men of affairs to an acknowledgement of their Maker. We also get speeches about *Lady Chatterley's Lover* and its description of the sexual act as a kind of an act of communion.

Plainly and simply, however, the great ecclesiastical officers came to be among the magnates of the realm, they were expected to speak up on behalf of religion. When the turbulent barons of William Rufus sang *Te Deum* in the King's bedchamber at the appointment of St Anselm as Archbishop of Canterbury, they had a very clear conception of the latter's function. Their successors were led by Stephen Langton in the path of right, to the establishment of Magna Carta, and many other instances could be given where spiritual and moral leadership came from the Primate. It has been only with the vast growth of worldliness in the last two centuries that the position

---

* For details about the peers spiritual see *A Constitutional History of the House of Lords* by L. O. Pike.

has radically changed. Yet when, with the nation sinking into a slough of complacency, the leaders of the national church should be recalling the people to higher things, as often as not their speeches are about Cyprus, European Union and other mundane matters.

The presence of religious leaders among the peers cannot be justified unless, indeed, they speak of religion and bring its basic truths home to all and sundry. It has been said that the Lords will listen to a bishop if he knows what he is talking about, and if he has not a sermon disguised in his speech. But that consideration should not weigh with a churchman. When he speaks in the House he should have ever in his mind that he is a spokesman for his Master, Jesus Christ. The praise or dispraise of temporal lords should be the last consideration. He should have the same steadfast courage in a spiritual, which worldly men show in a material cause. *Delenda est Carthago* were the words with which Cato the Censor concluded every speech which he made in the Senate of Rome. Derided at first, then doubtless labelled as a bore, Cato at length succeeded in his objective – to instil into the collective mind of Rome his own hatred of Carthage, until a generation grew up which accepted as automatic the necessity for the destruction of Carthage. Cannot the Primate of all England do in a just and holy cause what a pagan 200 years before Christ performed in a wicked one?

The reflection on the presence of the episcopal peers, if such I may term them, in our Second Chamber brings to the front the matter of the Established Church. This is the Establishment with a capital E, in the true meaning of the word. Enormous misconceptions abound as to the nature of the establishment of religion in this country. Many, very many people are of the opinion that the State pays the clergy's stipends. This is, indeed, the case with some established Churches in other lands, but it is not so in England. Only those clerics who are directly engaged on some business for the State, such as chaplains to the armed forces or the chaplains in the prison establishment receive their emoluments from the State. The overwhelming majority of the clergy of the Established Church are paid (a) from endowments, which are the gifts of faithful members of the Church, most of whom are dead, and from Queen Anne's Bounty, or (b) from money given in collections and other offerings at present being collected.

The State does very considerably interfere in the affairs of the Church, first in the appointment of her principal pastors, and, secondly, in a very real way by preventing her from developing along certain lines. There is enormous diversity in the form of the services in the English Church. This is due to the feeling that, rightly or wrongly, the Common Prayer Book of 1662 is not acceptable to the majority of people. In order to get over this difficulty, the authorities of the Church spent twenty years in revising the Prayer Book. They presented the results of their labours to the House of Commons, by whom the Deposited Book, as it was called, was twice rejected. The resultant chaos and lack of uniformity in the services of the Church is directly due to the interference of the State, and this through a Parliament composed, not of Anglicans, but of persons of all kinds of, and no, religious belief.

Then again many activities in churches are ultimately controlled through secular courts. In order to put an ornament in a church or to alter a church building a faculty must be obtained from the Provincial Courts of Canterbury (the Court of the Arches) and York (Chancery Court of York) of which the Dean of the Arches is the judge. From these Courts appeal may be made to the Judicial Committee of the Privy Council, so that secular judges have the last word in settling the law relating to Church usages. An example comes to hand (reported in *The Times* of 5 February 1962) from the Consistory Court of Coventry. A man who was a Roman Catholic was buried, with the full assent of his priest, in a Church of England parish churchyard. His wife who was an Anglican wished to put on the tombstone the words, 'Pray for the repose of the soul of. . . .' The Rector of the church objected the case. It was decided by the Chancellor of the Court that prayers for the dead are lawful in the Church of England. The inscription could be made, as the widow wished. Thus a layman in the church (albeit a judge) decided a point of Anglican theology.

Incidentally, this case illustrates the somewhat ludicrous position that a person who is not an Anglican has the right to be buried in an Anglican churchyard. By common law the freehold of the churchyard belongs to the rector, but the parishioners have the right to be buried therein, though the actual part for the grave is at the discretion of the rector and churchwardens. A clergyman can be prosecuted in the ecclesiastical court for refusing to bury a dissenter; moreover, by the Burial Laws Amendment Act, 1880, a person may be buried with an Anglican or any other religious service, provided due notice has been given to the incumbent. It may be recalled that David Lloyd George, as a young Welsh solicitor, made his first claim to fame by fighting cases for Welsh dissenters who wished to be buried in churchyards (the Welsh Church was not disestablished until 1920). 'Bury them by force' was his advice!

Does the Anglican Church gain any corresponding value from her association with the State, to counter-balance the serious disadvantages already mentioned? No doubt a large number of persons who pay only casual homage to religion give the right of first refusal to the Established Church, merely because she is felt in a vague sense to belong to them. In a recent survey of religious life in England, it was stated that out of 40 millions of people, only 27 millions were baptised in the Church of England. This is a low percentage but I am sure that it would be still lower if the Church were disestablished.

On the other hand, the disestablishment of the Church would slough off once and for all a large number of vague Anglicans whose grasp of their religious principles is nebulous. The Roman Catholic Church in England is small (though growing), but she has an influence quite out of proportion to her numbers. Let anyone try to get a criticism of the Roman Catholics into any popular paper. The Roman Catholic Church in England is united with a firm understanding on the part of all practising members as to the principles of the Faith. The leaders of English Roman Catholicism have succeeded in conveying the impression that they alone are qualified or entitled to speak for orthodox Christianity. A few years ago, at Easter a play was televised by the B.B.C., in which Christ was referred to by His Mother as being dead. The whole impression conveyed was that He had been a failure. Next day it was left to the Cardinal Archbishop of Westminster to thunder against this travesty of the life of Christ broadcast at the most sacred season of the Christian year. Where were the prelates of the Established Church?

If, therefore, the Church of England were disestablished and her numbers shrank, she might, by casting off the shoals of nominal members, become an active powerful body. I cannot see that on balance there is the slightest value in keeping up the Establishment. If it acted as it did up to 1600, or even to 1700, in maintaining the religious life of the country, it would have ample justification. But it is simply not helping to do anything to further the recovery of the spiritual bases of our civilisation which we have lost.

When talk is heard from time to time of reforming the House of Lords, there is usually mention of enriching (a splendid word for a vague thing) the debates in the Lords by bringing in representatives of the other communions beside the Anglican. The only result would be a vast increase in debate and the strife of contrary opinions.

England has long ceased to be a Christian country. If the Church authorities (and by these I mean the Anglican leaders) mean to be taken seriously when they talk of the conversion of England, they should begin by severing the State connection. A bold decisive step of this nature would impress the grossly materialistic world far more than any amount of preaching in wishy-washy undecided vagueness. If it should be objected that for a coronation the Church's rites are necessary, I should emphatically agree. I should point out, however, that a couple can be married in a register office as well as in a Church; the advantage of the second ceremony being the spiritual blessing from the Church. Just so, the Sovereign succeeds to the throne by primogeniture. The hallowing comes later from the Church. That service could easily be preserved.

Meantime, we have the melancholy spectacle of the Church taking a firm line on only one subject, divorce and remarriage while a partner is living. For this Edward VIII was to abdicate, and Princess Margaret to renounce Peter Townsend. I agree with the principle, but in the meantime there are other matters where the Church preserves a careful silence or is at best little removed from ambiguity. Apartheid in South Africa, the possession of nuclear weapons, the secularisation of education, the decay of honesty, the growth of cruelty, the denial of the most elementary truths about God and Christ – these are all matters where the New Testament speaks so very clearly, and where our spiritual lords seem so ineffective.

I suppose divorce is easier to handle.

CHAPTER SIX

The Landed Gentry

THE titled aristocracy is only like the mountain peaks of a mighty range which is submerged beneath the ocean. One of the peculiarities which distinguishes the British from any other titled system is the absence of titles from half the members of the Establishment, the ruling caste, or the few, however we choose to call them. After describing the peers, the baronets, the knights and so on, we cannot ignore the great number of gentlemen who have no titles. Perhaps their position is best summed up in the phrase, used so ably by Sir Bernard Burke, the 'untitled aristocracy'. At the end of the Table of Precedence come two classes – Esquires and Gentlemen. Both are definite social ranks. The esquire was created by the sovereign in just the same way as a peer or knight was made. As late as the end of the nineteenth century Queen Victoria created her faithful servant John Brown as an esquire. To this very day when a grant of armorial bearings is made, it carries with it the title of esquire, because the recipient of the letters patent is styled esquire in the document, and because the possession of arms gives one the outward and visible marks of gentility.

It may be doubted whether there is anywhere else in Europe a similar large class which has all the attributes of aristocracy save that of a title. Certainly there has been a great deal of confusion abroad as to the nature of our landed gentry and no little muddling at home. In European countries all the members of a noble family, including their descendants, bear titles and are correctly described as noble. This helps to account for the very large numbers of counts and countesses, barons and baronesses, in fact of princes and princesses, whom one meets. The fall of so many European empires and kingdoms has of course made easy the progress of impostors whose bogus titles have won them temporary positions in countries far from their own.

Most emphatically this is not the case with the British nobility. An outstanding example is the fact that during the greater part of his life, until, indeed, he received the Garter, Sir Winston Churchill was

64

plain Mr Winston Churchill. He was the grandson of a Duke of Marlborough, but his father was only a younger son. As such, Lord Randolph Churchill bore only a courtesy title, and in accordance with English social usage, his son in turn was merely an esquire and as such addressed as plain Mister. By contrast, Sir Winston's successor, Sir Anthony Eden (now Lord Avon), is a descendant of a Count of the old Holy Roman Empire (dissolved in 1806). He could therefore, be correctly styled Count Anthony Eden.

The British titled system seems expressly designed to allow for the fading off into obscurity of younger sons. For one generation they bear titles by courtesy. Then their descendants are indistinguishable from the great mass of the people. They are free to go out and found their own branches of the family.

The landed gentry themselves have not been backward in recognising their own importance. When I was editing the Burke volumes, I used sometimes to receive letters from people who described themselves as members of His or Her Majesty's Landed Gentry. Needless to remark, no such title has ever existed outside the soaring imagination of these correspondents. Still, a book as large as, or in some editions larger than, the *Peerage*, was required to record the untitled grades. This was *Burke's Landed Gentry* which between 1836 and 1952 went through seventeen editions. Nor is it the only work to take notice of the landed families. Until 1920 there were many editions of *Walford's County Families* in which the titled and the untitled appeared on the same pages, and in the same categories. It is true also that in *Kelly's Handbook to the Titled, Landed and Official Classes* the untitled landed gentry are listed along with the titled.

I think it would be true to say that there are more truly notable families among the landed gentry than among the peerage. Turning the pages of *Burke's Landed Gentry*, I have often been impressed by the names I found. Darwin, Speke, Winwood Reade, Pusey, Shakespeare, Haig, Disraeli, Horace Round, to mention only a very few, each most notable in his own sphere, are recorded somewhere in the *Landed Gentry*.

In order to understand how the untitled aristocracy came to be, we must understand the nature of the British titled system. How can people like the Earl of Dalkeith or Lord Lambton sit in the House of Commons, while entry therein is denied to Viscount Stansgate? The answer is that the latter is a peer, having succeeded his father, while the former are heirs to peerages. Dalkeith is heir to the Duke of

C

Buccleuch, Lambton to the Earl of Durham. The titles which these
gentlemen bear are purely of courtesy. They are the lesser titles of
their fathers. It is not generally realised that the higher the degree
of a peer in the peerage, the more titles he is likely to possess. Some
of the dukes have more than a dozen peerages. This being so, it has
become customary to call an eldest son of a peer above the rank of
viscount by one of the subsidiary titles of the father. Sometimes in
past generations and in formal documents it was the practice to
describe a peer's heir as the Hon. Charles Stuart, commonly called
Viscount Linton. If anyone wished to be very rude, he could, I suppose,
refer to the Earl of Dalkeith as Mr or the Hon. (though this is only
a courtesy term) Montagu-Douglas-Scott. It could be technically
correct. Usages are, however, established over centuries and generations. We all like our titles, even if they are only Mr, Mrs, Miss or
Master. There is no more validity (if as much) in these titles than in
those of the nobility.

Anyway, the radical difference between the Continental nobility
where all are titled, and the British where only the reigning peer has a
real title, accounts for the large recruitment of the landed gentry from
the peerage. Peerage families, through their younger scions, con-
tinually slip back into the landed gentry from which they have often
emerged. The Duke of Norfolk, though he has no son, has numerous
heirs to his title among his kinsfolk; most of these members of the
ducal Howard line are without title.

There can be no doubt that the British landed gentry have served
their country well. They have bled for her in many wars, they have
worked for her in all manner of causes, they have given an immense
amount of voluntary service. Man for man, family for family, they
have been far more useful to England than any remotely corresponding
body in a European country has been to its homeland.

Now the landed gentry is finished. What we see as we study England
is only the wreckage of the former class of squires and lairds. I suppose
few people have had more definite proof of the fade-out of the landed
gentry than I have. Over the period of twenty-five years during which
I was concerned with the publication, *Burke's Landed Gentry*, I saw
the steady, inexorable spread of landlessness among the former great
families. This was shown in a very simple but efficacious manner.
In the days of Sir Bernard Burke (he died in 1892) and right up to the
1914 war, it was necessary to possess some 2,000 acres to qualify for
admission to the volume. After that war, in the 1921 edition a number

of entries appeared with the word 'late' or 'formerly' of the old family property. Up to 1935 when I first worked on the book, there was still an effort to maintain 300 acres as a necessary possession for entry. In fact the 1937 Centenary edition stepped up very considerably the number of the landless. There was a further very large extension in the 1952 issue, which might be termed the definitive edition. Even when families still appear as of the property, they frequently own only a small fraction of the old estate. Some owners have succeeded in letting their mansions on favourable terms. They live in cottages but nurse what is left of the property with the hope of one day returning to some resemblance of their former splendour.

Nothing has been done to ameliorate the condition of the landed families. While agriculture is recognised as one of the main props of the country and receives subsidies from the Government, whether Conservative or Labour, nothing is proposed to make the lot of the landed proprietor more endurable. If a landowner is a tycoon and has industrial resources, then he can pull through. He can run his estate as a model, and his landed property becomes a hobby, just like yachting or the collection of antiques. This is completely removed from the conception and function of a landed aristocracy. When the landed gentry really flourished in this country, they were the centre of useful and cultural life in their districts. They gave employment and provided a valuable social service. They staffed the bench of justices, and the parish church, while most enterprises owed something to their leadership.

Today this position has been completely reversed. The wealthy business man is no substitute for the family which lived for generations in the district. Another fact of very serious consequence is that the peerage is decreasingly recruited from the county families, so that our titled system is cut off from its proper soil. This is depriving the peerage and the honours system of any stable basis. Aristocracy wherever it has flourished, has had its roots in the soil. Now the old landed gentry class has been reduced to an enfeebled condition where it can no longer supply either a social and cultural centre in a district, or produce rulers and leaders. I think that this fact is the worst feature of the whole Establishment situation, because it means that the natural recruiting ground of the titled few has been destroyed, and that titles are, therefore, *in vacuo*, without a supporting class.

It may be argued that the families which once owned land and are now unlanded, may still have influence in the community by reason

of their pedigrees. True, in many quarters there are those who cling
to the only reminder which they possess of their former status. But
a pride in their own pedigrees, while it may preserve individuals, will
not give back the county leadership which can come only from
physical presence in a place. A family such as the Okeovers of Okeover
(I have deliberately chosen one which is extinct in the male line) with
900 years' tenure of their lands, were a force in their own neighbour-
hood. If, as has happened in so many cases, they had been compelled
to sell their property, they could have retained their family pride and
honour, but their usefulness in the country would have been gone.

In saying that nothing has been done for the benefit of the landed
families, I am not unmindful of the grants which are made from the
Exchequer for the upkeep of historic homes, nor forgetful of the
work of the National Trust. In the former case, the grants will sometimes assist an owner to stay in his ancestral home, but not to preserve
his estate. The excellent work of the National Trust is dependent upon
funds which must be provided by a property-owner desirous of passing
his property to the Trust. In short, he must have funds sufficient to
endow the property before he can disembarrass himself of it. That
being the case, it will be some considerable time before any financial
easement comes to the family exchequer. Moreover, the Trust is bound
to be impersonal, and thus the reverse of the personal ownership
which has done so much for our countryside. I feel that the saddest
sights are those of National Trust property where the former owner
has retained the right to live in the old home for a generation or
maybe two.

It is possible that the county families could have pulled through
but for the oncoming of the Second World War. Robert Henriques,
in his fine novel, *Through the Valley*, gives the development as it
occurred between the wars. I have known personally several families,
and, of course, learned of scores of others, who were just beginning
to pick up in the mid-1930s. Then their struggles were ended by the
onset of war. Quite apart from the new financial burdens which the
1939 war entailed, there was a revolution in Britain which removed
the possibility of servants, and of labourers on the estate. In one
instance in a house and property which required a staff of forty,
there were only three employees in 1950. Of these, one was a butler, a
youth awaiting call up!

But, of course, it will be argued that these changes were inevitable
when the Welfare State had to be set up and social justice brought

into what one politician described as the mess of centuries. In fact
nothing in the ruin of the landed has had anything to do with the
betterment of the lot of those living in slum conditions. These conditions were the product of the Industrial Revolution, of the profiteer,
the Manchester School, the whole attitude of *laissez-faire*, and they
led directly to the growth of Socialism. In the Industrial Revolution
very little regard was paid to the sufferings of the human beings
whose work made Britain's economic supremacy possible. Anyone
who approaches one of our great cities by rail will see Victorian (and
earlier) slums which make one wonder how human beings could ever
have felt comfortable while other human beings lived in them. Though
it is true that there are cases where large areas of what are now
urban slum property formerly belonged to a county family, it
will invariably be found that this family was of very recent origin.
In his novel *Rape of the Fair Country* Alexander Cordell, describing
the development of an iron works in a Welsh valley, names a landed
gentry family. But the fact that he gives it only a short pedigree proves
my point. The old families, such as those listed in Shirley's *Noble and
Gentle Men of England*, had nothing to do with slum development. It
is not their fault that the modern tycoon has chosen to assume the
mantle of 'landed proprietor'.

CHAPTER SEVEN

Paradoxes of the Titled System

THUS far I have been describing our system of title from Crown to Coronets, from Duke to Esquire, without attempting what may be termed its rationale. Why titles at all, it may be asked. Can a human being be so important in the affairs of this small planet, that he should be dignified and distinguished as His Majesty, His Grace, His Holiness? Surely not. For even the most important of V.V.I.P.s has not yet discovered how to be superior to the requirements of food, drink, sleep and the toilet; much less can anyone escape the levelling hand of death. Nothing can save the eminent from the same fate as the obscure. One of the criticisms which may legitimately be levelled against our Nordic (Protestant) culture is that by abolishing or disregarding the correct Western European (Catholic) Christian attitude to death, it has helped to deify mankind. A conspiracy is found in most Protestant countries to avoid mention of death, and to have on behalf of the dead, in place of a requiem for the soul of the deceased, a memorial service. At these curious functions, the philosophically-minded listener may be excused for wondering if the Twelve Apostles and other most eminent saints of Christendom do not take very secondary place to the merits of the memorialised departed. Some of those who are thus commemorated are described in the language of moral hyperbole. No hint is given that the dead man possessed any faults, and, of course, no reference is ever made to the deceased having merely anticipated the living in going forward to an inevitable judgment.

Viewed in this way against the background of humanity's faults and fate, the use of titles is indefensible. Even shifting from philosophical to democratic considerations, it is hard to see how titles can be justified, at least at first sight, in a democratic state. The titles of the clergy are, I think, plainly out of keeping with Christ's clear commands. But the unity of Christendom on the honorific titles to be borne by the various ranks of clerics is as impressive as its disunity on matters of theological doctrine. Roman Catholic and Presbyterian, Anglican and Greek Orthodox, Baptist and Wesleyan bear an ecumenical testimony to the necessity of evading Christ's instructions: 'So it shall not be among you'.

Can any good reasons be advanced against the clear-cut objections to titles? One plea of great force is that titles have been and are being used among all nations. This is true even in countries like the U.S.A., where titles of nobility are expressly forbidden to the citizens. There is an enormous proliferation in America of the type of distinction which does not proceed from a Crown. I find a letter waiting for me which bears on its heading 'Office of the Grand Secretary, Masonic Temple – '. The Grand Secretary is one of the high offices of the Grand Lodge of Ancient Free and Accepted Masons of one of the American States. Now, admittedly, there are Masons and Masonic titles in plenty in England, but there would rarely be such an elaborate and somewhat ostentatious heading to notepaper. In the U.S.A. Masonry has a vast membership and I think that its various titles do provide an outlet for a human instinct which is released in England more easily by our honours system. Again, there is, not only in the U.S.A. but in Europe also, a very widespread system of doctorates. I do not know how many times I have been addressed from abroad as 'Dr Pine'. Large numbers of Americans have this appellation, hence they conclude that their corresponding number in Britain is also thus distinguished. In European politics everyone is 'Dr'. I notice this usage applies very much to the worthies of that handful of countries such as Uruguay, Switzerland and Indonesia, where honours of the British type are eschewed.

It seems indeed that the interest in titles is universal. It is better to keep it within some sensible bounds, as where the titles can come only from a sovereign. I incline to be very suspicious of regimes or persons who criticise our British system, when I find their citizens tuft-hunting after honours as grimly as anyone in our country.

Even in the Communist world, honours are firmly established. Russia, and every state which has imitated her, has instituted orders and decorations. These are not in accordance with Marx's principles. In Russia there has even been a renovation of some old Tsarist orders. There was the Order of St Alexander Nevsky. This commemorated a great hero of medieval Russia. Under the Soviets it was remodelled. The Saint disappeared from the title but the Order of Alexander Nevsky is now very much in use in the U.S.S.R. In addition, the old Marshal Suvorov, of former Tsarist days, is now remembered by an Order of Chivalry. It has been found that an appeal merely to utilitarian or materialistic motives is not enough. The Russians require an incentive of a more exalted kind, just as other people do in order to make the greatest efforts.

With some minds this incentive is simply and solely a matter of vanity. In general though, it is, I think, inspired by the desire of recognition, of appreciation by those among whom one dwells. From the other side, that of the bestowers of honours, there is the more mundane consideration that honours are of infinitesimal cost to the State. Even the most beautiful gold medal, or the most resplendent chivalric insignia cannot compare for a moment with the cost of an annual pension, especially if the latter should be weighed in its true worth and be substantial. If a peerage be granted as the fair return for a lifetime's work in public service, then the recipient has to pay and not the donor. The trimmings of a peerage, robes, coronet, coat-of-arms, notepaper, coronet on car, etc., etc., can easily run up to £500–£1,000. The State merely issues the letters patent, as part of the work of its heraldic establishment. This was what Oliver Goldsmith meant in remarking that European sovereigns had found it an excellent recompense for the loss of arms and legs to bestow in exchange some pretty bits of coloured ribbon. It is when we come to hereditary titles that the matter is different. They are very much a relic of a feudal past, and for that reason they have disappeared from almost every country in Europe. Feudalism has gone, and so have these appendages of it. England is so much more truly conservative than any other country that it has kept these strange survivals longer than anywhere else. In other countries, the hereditary title lives on, as in Sweden or France, but as a private affair. In England it is part of the legislature.

No other country has shown such remarkable skill in adapting its ancient institutions to the changing needs of centuries. But has the time come for a more fundamental change? It is often said that the experience of three hundred years ago confirmed the British people in their feelings about revolution. I have cited their devotion to the monarchy in the past three centuries as proof of their horror at the execution of Charles I. I believe this to be true, but even so the full nature of the Cromwellian revolution needs to be analysed. The Great Rebellion or the Civil War began as a struggle between Crown and Parliament over the control of taxation. Underneath this were several other matters, notably the religious controversy between prelatist and Puritan. In the end, as in all real revolutions, a small

minority gained control. They were led by Cromwell. In 1642 when
the Civil War began, no one contemplated the King's death. By 1649
the fierce extremists who formed the Army were ready for anything.
The Church had already been purged of prelacy and the Archbishop
of Canterbury, Laud, sent to the block. In January 1649, Charles I
was executed after a trial which could not have possessed any legality.
Charles refused to plead since the Court had no authority, and in
this he was undoubtedly right. One of the long-term results of his
trial and condemnation was that the law itself was brought into
disrepute. One of the more immediate consequences came a few days
after the King's execution. There was passed an Act for the abolition
of the House of Peers. In less than three hundred plain, strong words,
the House of Lords was cleared away from the national scene. The
terms of the Act are worth a wider audience: 'The Commons of
England assembled in Parliament, finding by too long experience
that the House of Lords is useless and dangerous to the People of
England to be continued, have thought fit to Ordain and Enact,
and be it Ordained and Enacted by this present Parliament and by the
Authority of the same, that from henceforth the House of Lords in
Parliament, shall be and is hereby wholly abolished and taken away,
and that the Lords shall not from henceforth meet or sit in the said
House called The Lords' House, or in any other House or Place
whatsoever as a House of Lords, etc.'

In all this, as in the trial of the King, the Parliament or rather the
House of Commons claimed to be acting for the people of England.
The great groan which followed the King's execution in Whitehall
was their commentary on this claim. The vast majority of the people
did not want the King to die. But they were not truly represented by
the Parliament which had sat for several years, and was shortly to be
purged and reduced in numbers. Crown and Lords had been abolished,
so had the prelates. The Puritans controlled the Church. The Army
was the only effective force and Cromwell's power rested on it. The
turn came next of the House of Commons; it was driven out and the
Government of England was in the hands of one man ruling by
military force.

Then there was a strange revolution. Cromwell found it very hard
to govern without the familiar framework of the State. He tried to
secure an elected Parliament; he tried to create another House; above
all he sought by fairly open ways to become king. I do not doubt that
he would have accepted the title and position of monarch but for

C*

the opposition of his soldiers. They quite understandably refused to put up the House of Cromwell in place of that of Stuart. It was from the Army that there came the stirring of equality and democracy. Long before the equalitarian impulses of the French Revolution, the same feelings appeared in England. The ordinary soldiers wished to have the vote for all, with a properly elected Parliament, in short a real democracy. They thought that because there had been revolution in the State, with the overturning of so many ancient institutions, there would be a further revolution which would bring about a representative Parliament in England. This was the movement which expressed itself through the small bodies, the well-known Diggers, and the Levellers. But these aspirations were destined to fail. A great deal of Cromwell's time and energy as Protector was taken up in repressing any movement towards genuine democracy among his troops. The theory has been advanced that the overthrow of the monarchy had been the work of the gentry, and that they were not content until they had succeeded in getting their own republic with one of their number as its permanent head. And certainly Cromwell did come from the class of smaller gentry. His family was armigerous and landed, some branches were wealthy, and all shared the same type of education. But what the gentry wanted was not democracy but oligarchy. To persons of such position and influence it was quite unthinkable that they should give equality to a class beneath them.*

Democracy failed to materialise, the imitations of the old institutions also failed. The only alternative was to bring back the former regime. For the first time in England's history the Establishment adapted itself to changed circumstances. On a very rapid superficial reading of the seventeenth century, the Roundheads or Puritans failed in their aims. Their dead opponent, Charles I, proved, like Julius Caesar, mighty yet, and in the restoration of his son the Cavaliers triumphed. Yet the monarchy would never be the same again. In the very first Parliament of Charles II's reign, when loyalty prompted the vote of a large sum of money to the King, there was also voted the abolition of the feudal tenures. The feudal dues, the claims for which had largely helped to cause the Civil War, were quietly dropped. By the great skill of Charles II an open rupture was averted, but with James II on the throne, the old conflict was renewed. Very shortly, in 1688–89, came the Glorious Revolution. From thence

* For a further account of Cromwell's place in English history, see Appendix IV.

an oligarchy ruled in England. It did not suit that class to pursue the reforms which had been initiated under the Commonwealth. The use of English in the Law Courts in place of Norman French did not come until 1734. No other university arose beside Oxford and Cambridge until the nineteenth century. Some old courts, the Star Chamber, and the High Commission were abolished and never revived, but otherwise the legal system with its absurd arrangements of two kinds of justice was allowed to drag on until 1876. The reforming impulse of the seventeenth century found no renewal until another 200 years had passed.

In the period from 1689 to 1832 the aristocracy ruled. They were the natural leaders of the nation against Napoleon, but there were movements from the last quarter of the eighteenth century onwards which made it impossible for them to retain their leadership. The Industrial Revolution greatly increased the wealth of the country; it brought a new class of wealthy men to a parity with the old landowning interest. These were the new capitalists and employers, but as they mostly wanted the same things from their money – land, family, gentility – as the older squires and lords, they were generally accepted after a couple of generations. The son of one of the new wealthy – Sir Robert Peel – became the Tory leader and Prime Minister. The older Establishment absorbed the new leaders and made them into passable imitations of the old.

So far it was another example of the successful adaptation of the Establishment. Then came the political agitation to reform the system of the rotten boroughs, in short to make Edmund Burke's quaint conception of democracy bear some resemblance to reality. There was fierce agitation in the country, and out of it came the Reform Bill of 1832. The net result of this, in actual concession to voting powers, was to bestow the franchise on some 500,000 persons. The purpose of the agitation, however, had been much more than just to achieve such a balanced state of affairs, with an electorate of property-owning highly responsible persons, and once more the forces of democracy broke out in the Chartist Movement. The Chartists demanded suffrages for all at twenty-one, secret ballots, payment of M.P.s, and so on, all of which reforms have come about slowly over many decades.

As an immediate force Chartism failed, the second great failure of democracy. Had democracy won through in either the mid-seventeenth or early nineteenth century, the course of our history would have been much happier. Because of the failure of democracy to achieve success under the Commonwealth, there came all the hardships of the Enclosure Acts in the eighteenth century. Because Chartism failed, there was a perpetration of the miseries of the Industrial Revolution, with the result that Socialism and Communism came eventually in the field to push the cause of the underdog. A militant trade unionism, closely allied with one school of political thought, was to arise. This could hardly have happened had there been a Parliament elected on anything approaching universal suffrage, but right up to the 1914 war this country still possessed a minority Government. After 1918, however, the framework of the Establishment was stretched to breaking point. It has been no longer possible over the past forty-five years to pretend to assimilate everyone into the Establishment. You cannot turn 50 millions into squires, lairds and aristocrats. You cannot give them all the same training.

The Establishment has, therefore, begun to break up. Here a little, there a little, a reform in one direction, an abolition in another, it all amounts to a rapid reduction of the idea of the Establishment. The conception of an Establishment is that of the management of the many-headed multitude by the skilled few. When the majority have political power, and use it in an educated manner, they will not submit to being pushed and pulled about by a few superior persons. It is becoming every year more difficult to get away with manœuvres of the Wedgwood Benn or the Guildford Cathedral variety – of which more later.

Thus far it might be thought that I am writing an *Apologia pro Doctrina Populi* but, unfortunately, democracy is not developing in England into the rule of the people. In a general election it is considered a heavy poll if there is a total vote of 82 per cent of the electorate. This means that nearly 20 per cent of our electors do not vote at all. The poll is usually smaller, even at general elections; in by-elections polls of 60 per cent are good or normal, while in local government elections the percentage of voters is very frequently 40 per cent or below. All this adds up to a lack of interest in civic responsibility which is a most serious phenomenon. A greater threat, however, is the fact that since the end of the last war the voters have demonstrated beyond a peradventure that the matter which more than anything else interests them is their own material welfare. The overwhelming success of the Socialists in 1945 sprang from the horror of unemployment and of social insecurity. When the Conservatives returned to power, they promised freedom from restrictions and this included freedom from the various forms of rationing. Because an ever-increasing flow of goods went to the mass of families throughout the country, the Conservatives were returned in 1955 and 1959.

So long as democracy – so different from the version practised in classical Athens – functions in this manner, the Establishment, stretched though it may be, has little to fear. Until comparatively recent days everyone knew what 'The Establishment' meant. It was the group of people at the top who from long tradition controlled the country's destinies. But today in theory those destinies are controlled by the mass of the people; in theory, too, there should be no need for 'The Establishment' at all. But it persists – or some would say lingers on – and, since it is pulled this way and that, trying to adapt itself to equivocal circumstances, no one knows exactly what it comprises.

Perhaps a common illustration may clarify the position. In business people often talk of what 'they' are going to do. By 'they' they mean the directors or other executives. In the end 'they' become almost impersonal, one might with as much propriety talk of 'it'. This is the attitude of many intelligent people towards the leaders of the Establishment. Someone ought to get such a job, but will 'they' allow him to have it? Such vague references are strengthened when Archbishop Lord Fisher (in the Deanery of Guildford case) writes of the advisers of the Crown in Church matters. Who are these persons? Officially, the adviser of the Crown in matters of Church preferment is the Prime Minister, assisted by the Archbishop of Canterbury and any other bishops. But the impression created is of a 'great cloud of witnesses' whose identity is concealed and far from heavenly, yet who are able to intervene decisively.

For this reason it is often hard to define just who belong to the Establishment and who are merely outriders and hangers-on. Furthermore the modern usage of the word 'Establishment' simply does not assist us. Anyone who checks the words in the Oxford English Dictionary will find a round dozen of definitions. These range from such matter-of-fact explanations as: 'Action or means of establishing: fact of being established (in various senses of that verb)', to 'establishing by law (a church, religion, or form of worship)' or 'ecclesiastical system established by law' (more fully, 'Church Establishment'). There is also the meaning of an organised body of men, maintained by the State for a specific purpose, such as the military, naval or civil establishment. In this latter sense everyone who knows much of the armed forces or the Civil Service is familiar with the meaning of establishment. There is allowance on the establishment or staff of a particular section for two squadron leaders, and so on. But the only correct sense above in which Establishment is used in agreement with ultra-modern usage is that of the Church of England Establishment. 'A Clergyman of the Establishment' is an expression which had and still has its meaning.

Since the last war the word Establishment has come to mean something much beyond this, e.g. in *The Establishment, A Symposium* edited by Hugh Thomas (Blond, 1959), we have chapters covering the Public Schools, the Army, Parliament and the B.B.C., but while there is much wit and penetration in the respective studies, I do not think anyone is likely to know at the end of his reading, who are the persons who form the Establishment. In my study I have endeavoured to show the Establishment as culminating in the titled system which stems from the Crown. Thus we have Crown, Royal House, Lords (both Spiritual and Temporal); lesser titles: Baronets, Knights, Companions and other members of the various Orders of Chivalry. It has been necessary in order adequately to understand the system to go on to the large class of the landed gentry. I have described titles as the peaks of an extensive range. I have pointed out that British aristocracy is distinguished from that of European countries by the presence within it of a large class of untitled persons who are, nevertheless (to use the language of the market place), as good as the titled.

Now these persons, the aristocracy, titled and untitled alike, have for several centuries controlled certain professions: the Sacred Ministry (commonly known as the Church, among even the best educated), the Law, to some extent medicine; the armed forces, especially when until quite recently these were confined to the Army and the Navy; the City Livery companies; the higher education, as represented in the major public schools and the two ancient universities; and the higher reaches of such movements as Freemasonry.

These are the people who are fairly referred to as 'they', the powers-that-be and those with influence. Needless to say, their influence culminates in politics and administration. Business has never been controlled by them, at least not directly. But an indirect, yet decisive control has been exercised even in the sphere of commerce. It has been the peculiar genius of the English ruling class that, while opposing the growth of genuine equality and democracy, they have never prevented, but rather assisted the entry into their own ranks of an outstanding plebeian. As long ago as the fourteenth century the great family of Pole owed its origins to a successful war-contractor and moneylender. The De la Poles became Earls and Dukes of Suffolk within three or four generations and ranked as one of the greatest families in medieval England. The sneer of the ex-Kaiser Wilhelm II – 'I thought your King had been yachting with his grocer' (in reference to Edward VII and Sir Thomas Lipton) – showed a failure to understand the English mentality. In what may fairly be called the upper-class or public-school spirit, a fair fight is followed by no hard feeling. A man of the people has proved his worth, and fought his way into the inner ring. Very well, let's accept the fact; he's one of us. This principle has permitted the absorption down the ages of all sorts of persons into the circle of the governing class: unscrupulous Tudor lawyers and courtiers; wealthy men in the seventeenth and eighteenth centuries whose fortunes came from very doubtful sources; industrial revolutionists of the grim early nineteenth century; trade union leaders in the twentieth. All these have been transformed into more than passable imitations of an upper-class model. In passing, I may notice a strange fact. Among the English aristocracy there are very few really ancient pedigrees. Consequently, when anyone has tried to deflate a *novus homo*, it has often led to retorts which are embarrassing from their truth. The game has long since been given up. Just why settled England should produce few long pedigrees, in contrast with wild ravaged Ireland and Scotland, I do not know. I can only deduce from the evidence that in England there has often been a dearth of male heirs, with the result that the *parvenu* has been able to marry a wife of much longer recorded ancestry than himself. As pedigrees are usually traced in the male line, this means that in the reference books only a short account will appear, not much about the father's family, and a condensed reference to the mother's noble line.

Now, however, as I have said, since the forces of the universal franchise have become too powerful to be resisted, the numbers to be absorbed grow even greater, and the Establishment is stretched to the point where it breaks down.

As to the identity of 'they', those mysterious wielders of power, the two companion volumes, *Burke's Peerage* and *Burke's Landed Gentry* contain the names and particulars of at least 90 per cent of them. Of the remaining 10 per cent, it can safely be said that at least half of them will eventually find their way into one or both of these volumes. It would be easy for a critic to cull from modern society the names of half a dozen wealthy and influential men who have no title or estate. In each case a good reason can be found for the exclusion from the earthly paradise: a separation from his wife in one case; in another a shady transaction in early commercial life which he has not been able to suppress; sometimes (rarely) a genuine dislike of flummery, at others a deep-seated inferiority complex which would make him feel uncomfortable with a title.

The essence of the difficulties in which this established upper class finds itself today consists in three things: 1. The appearance of a very large and fiercely stirring educated class which is too big to be absorbed, as far as can be seen, into its traditions. This class, while numerous, is still too small to alter the materialism or indifference of the bulk of the voters. 2. The great change since 1939 in British influence in the world. It has become almost a chant of jubilation in some quarters to repeat that Britain is no longer a great power. This means that the tradition of a millennium as enshrined in the monarchy (which I have shown in Chapter Two) is broken or would be broken. The present time is a serious crisis in our fate. We must find a way to an alternative greatness, or, quite frankly, perish by gradual decline into starvation. 3. The class from which the Establishment was recruited, has been broken, partly by losses in war, which fell more heavily on an officer class than on any other, but even more by the operation of taxation which makes it impossible for long to retain a landed estate.

We thus reach a state when quite clearly the old Establishment is under severe criticism. It is in danger of breaking up; some parts of it ought to go, for they have become ridiculous or positively bad. Yet mere change will not help. A sense of spiritual and moral values must be brought back into our national life.

So far I have traced the outlines of the Establishment. I propose now to penetrate within, first with the Church, then the Law, Education, the Fighting Services, Commerce. To conclude, I shall survey the recording machine of the system, the College of Arms, and everything that it stands for.

CHAPTER EIGHT

The Church of England as by Law Established

IN Chapter Five I have dealt with the matter of the Spiritual Lords, the archbishops and bishops of the Church of England, and by consequence, with the Church of which they form the most (materially) distinguished part. But a much more precise study of the Church is necessary if we are to understand its part in, and the reasons why it must always be above, the Establishment.

Today there are some 14,000 Anglican clergy. The Anglican Communion is a world-wide organisation with dioceses not only outside England, but also in every continent. The Episcopal Church of the U.S.A. is in communion with Canterbury. The Anglican Communion is the leader and I think the mainstay in the widespread movement for re-union among the Christian bodies outside the Roman Catholic Church.

How has this position been attained? Largely, if not solely, through the dissemination of English political influence and the English language over the last few centuries. Otherwise the Church of England might well have resembled the Church of Sweden in its sphere of influence. Had the Swedish Empire endured, there might have been overseas Churches in communion with the mother Church of Sweden.

There is another feature of the English Church which is peculiar to itself, and that is the claim to continuity with the Church of England before the Reformation. I do not think that any other reformed communion makes this claim. It is certainly not so in Scotland or Germany, where the Reformed Church represents a body formed anew in the sixteenth century and separated by a clear break from the Papist or Romish Church.

This claim of the Anglican Church is clearly set out in the Prayer Book (last authoritatively revised in 1662). There is not the slightest sign or consciousness of a new Church having been created by Henry VIII, Edward VI, or Elizabeth I. The story goes that Pope Sixtus V was willing to accept the local peculiarities, such as services in the vernacular and a married clergy, had Queen Elizabeth been willing on her part, to accept Papal supremacy. This course of action would have been in accordance with Rome's policy as shown with the Uniat Churches which are in full communion with the Pope but retain their own peculiarities.

One of the most vulgar and silly remarks frequently heard is to the effect that the Church of England came into existence because of a divorce of Henry VIII. *Ut Ecclesia Anglicana libera sit*, is one of the clauses in Magna Carta. From very early times the English Church was often in opposition to the Papacy, not so much on grounds of faith as over matters of practice. The Norman Conquest (clearly an act of aggression) was aided and abetted by the Papacy, because it was known that the Normans would be more regular in payment of dues to Rome, and would bridle the independence of the English clergy. Yet even the first of the Norman kings, cruel and ruthless conqueror that he was, found it necessary to resist Papal exactions. He had many followers among the later English kings, but an exception was King John. At first he was threatened by the Pope Innocent III, but later when he submitted, Innocent took John under his protection. The barons who were in arms against John, then experienced the weight of the Pope's displeasure. John, meanwhile, in making his submission had agreed to hold his crown and realm as a fief from the Pope. As far as I know there was never a repudiation of this agreement, so that on a technicality England is a temporal fief of the Holy See.

No doubt the quarrels in Henry VIII's reign between the Crown and the Roman Pope, were motivated by personal desires, rather than by a wish to reform the Church. When the Pope had failed to meet Henry's wishes over the divorce from his Queen, and the breach had been completed, the English Church remained completely medieval in its outlook. A great change came with the publication of the Bible in English, but, otherwise, Henry was determined to keep Protestantism at bay. Not even he, however, could stay the forces which he had allowed to come to his aid. The Protestant Reformation followed, and the English Church became, in the words of Archbishop Fisher, both Catholic and Protestant.

It was intended that all the nation should continue in the same Church. The attempt to realise this ideal lasted for 100 years, but in 1662 it had to be given up. From that time until the present, large sections of the nation have been outside the national Church. A recent figure quoted was of 27 millions baptised in the Church of England out of a total population of 40 millions.

During the eighteenth century a spirit of lethargy descended upon the Church. A great deal of valuable energy was lost when the non-jurors left the fold in the beginning of William and Mary's reign. In the eighteenth century the power which John Wesley wielded was lost to the Church, owing to the obscurantism of its prelates, though Wesley himself stated that he died in the Communion of the Church of England.

The Church, in fact, in the early nineteenth century was almost dead. A devoted Christian, Dr Thomas Arnold of Rugby, declared that the Church as it then was, no human power could save.

In 1833 there began the famous Oxford Movement. The principal leaders were Pusey, Keble and Newman. The object of the movement was to awaken the Church to its heritage of Catholic doctrine. The term, Anglo-Catholic, began to be used. It was applied to those Anglican divines who from the time of Richard Hooker (1554–1600) had set out the claims and views of Anglican theology. Newman seceded to Rome in 1845. Many others followed his example; right up to our own time, Anglo-Catholicism or High Churchism has provided a useful bridge between England and Rome, as many pamphlets published by the (Roman) Catholic Truth Society bear witness.

The movement prospered and from doctrine went into practice. The churches were brightened up, vestments were worn, incense was burned, crucifixes and statues introduced. In the last 130 years the High Church or Anglo-Catholic movement has made vast progress. To take one example, in the sphere of social work which the Church had so much neglected, many self-sacrificing Anglo-Catholic priests gave themselves to schemes of social reform which were often frankly political. The beautiful church at Thaxted in Essex has become throughout a generation the centre of religious political teaching of a Socialist nature. In addition I think it not unfair to ascribe some share in the multiplication of dioceses both in England and abroad to the zeal of High Churchmen.

Today the Anglo-Catholic movement has lost force and is no longer the power which it was. Formerly it could boast leaders of national status like the late Earl of Halifax, who are now wanting in the movement. Then there was one of the most learned theologians in the Anglican Communion, if not the most, Dr Charles Gore, Bishop of Worcester, Birmingham and Oxford, as the leading Anglo-Catholic divine. Dr Darwell Stone, another High Churchman, was the foremost patristic scholar of the time. There was the very scholarly work, *Essays Catholic and Critical*; and in a more popular sphere there were the great Anglo-Catholic Congresses which filled the Albert Hall. But these things are matters of thirty years back.

For some 300 years the Ministry of the Church was in the hands of the upper classes. This has led to the loss of spiritual power. With the growth of education, the creation of more universities, and the growth of the Anglican Communion in lands such as Canada, there has come a widening in the education and social class of candidates for the Church's Ministry and with it the chance to regain lost ground. At one time as I know well from the study of numerous pedigrees it was possible, on discovering that an ancestor was an Anglican clergyman, to be fairly sure that he was also a graduate of Oxford or Cambridge. Today it would be rash to assume that an Anglican priest was a member of any university.

Yet with all the broadening out of social classes in recruitment for the Ministry, the heads of the ecclesiastical Establishment remain much the same. Out of the forty-three diocesan bishops of England, only one, I believe, is a London University graduate. The Spiritual Lords thus grow more and more out of touch with their much more numerous under-clergy. Many of our archbishops and bishops have been schoolmasters or dons. Very few of them have had parochial experience. A great gulf opens between them and their clergy. There is great dissatisfaction on the part of the latter. Here, most noticeably, the machinery of the Establishment creaks and groans on its way to breaking up.

A prime example of this tendency occurred in 1961 with the affair of the Deanery of Guildford. Briefly, the Provost of the Cathedral was not appointed to the Deanery when the Cathedral was completed. There was a great outcry and agitation on the part of the Church people in the diocese. The matter was aggravated by the fact that the Provost had resigned – that is, he had been allowed to resign – his living, in the clear expectation that he would be appointed as Dean. When it was known that he was not to be so appointed, the then Archbishop of Canterbury (now Lord Fisher of Lambeth), explained that the Queen's advisers knew all about the matter. He did not explain who these advisers were. To crown the ineptitude of the whole proceeding, at the very time when a petition on behalf of the Provost was being presented to the Queen, it was announced that the new Dean had been appointed. There could hardly have

been a more calculated manner of exhibiting contempt or disregard
for the processes of public opinion and of Church democracy. That
it was not calculated, may be conceded. But no sophistry can overcome the conclusion which may legitimately be drawn. The powers
behind the scenes, the mysterious 'they' had completely ignored the
wishes of the public. The whole matter was arranged without the
slightest regard for what people might want, nor was any concern
shown for the feelings of the unfortunate Provost, or for that matter
for his prospects when he had resigned. Now this is what is likely
to happen when the clerical Establishment is controlled as it is by
schoolmasters, dons and the like. It must be hard for even the best of
them to understand the problems of the majority of their clergy, who
have to fight the battle of the Church in their parishes. The schoolmaster bishops tend to be disciplinarian and autocratic in dealing
with clergy and laity. The university professors on the episcopal bench
are the persons in the Church mainly responsible for the movement of
'enrichment', of 'new visions of truth' and all the other curiously
ineffective compromises which mar the Church of England. No
improvement in fact is likely to come from mere disestablishment
as long as the same type of cleric remains in control.

The New Testament does not set out the views of schools of thought.
It deals with the 'faith once delivered to the saints', to use its own
language. In the Church of England there are diversities of view even
on fundamental doctrines. It is this aspect of the Established Church
which has bestowed their most powerful argument upon the Roman
Catholics in England. How can your Church, they say, represent
Christ's Church, when it speaks with divided voice even on some of
the cardinal doctrines in the creed?

Again, in the Church of England there is a great diversity of
practice. This makes church attendance very difficult for the ordinary
man or woman not skilled in the niceties of ecclesiastical usage. Will
it be Matins or Holy Communion at 11 a.m.? Whichever service it is,
will the form used be that of the 1662 book or of 1928? Or will it be
of the vicar's own spiritual concoction? Both Low and High Church
are equally to blame, for all shades of opinion in the Church are
adding to the lack of uniformity in the services.

Should not the Church regulate its own affairs? It has endeavoured
to do so and has been prevented by the State. In 1919 the Church
Assembly, a species of Church Parliament, was set up by the Parliament of Westminster. Ostensibly the object of this exercise was to

allow the Church to govern itself. In practice it was simply a device
to disburden the House of Commons of any unnecessary trouble over
Church measures in which it was not interested. The sanction of
Parliament is still necessary for any measures passed by the Church
Assembly. That sanction is not forthcoming when the measure
interests the House of Commons. For many years it was known that
virtual anarchy existed in the services. The Common Prayer Book
of 1662 was not being obeyed. It was argued that if the book were
revised, and an improved new Prayer Book produced, this would
have the force of law. Anyone who disregarded the new Prayer Book
would then be a law-breaker and could be proceeded against by the
bishops. Twenty years' labour went into the 1928 Prayer Book. All
to no avail, the Book was twice rejected by the House of Commons.
The liturgical chaos in the Church is now worse than ever. No prospect of righting it is remotely in sight.

Since the war some considerable advance has been made as
regards the Church's finances. These are now far more in order than
they have been for centuries. But apart from this the progress of the
Church in its vital work is constantly hindered because it is controlled
by the State. 'Since its inception in 1919, four Church Assembly commissions have recommended changes in the ecclesiastical courts, and
at least three have asked for modification in the system of appointing
bishops, but things remain exactly what they were. Why? Because
the leaders of the Church establishment think that rows with Parliament are indecorous, if not positively indecent' (*Time and Tide*,
27 April 1961). To which I would merely add that the leaders of the
Establishment are akin in Church and State.

If disestablishment of the Church took place, then there would
be a chance of a change in the Church leaders. Most people know the
name of Father Trevor Huddleston. In England he would have lived
and died with the small fame of a celebrated preacher. Today he is
the Bishop of Masasi. They manage things differently in Africa.
Then, too, one can hardly imagine Joost de Blank, Archbishop of
Cape Town, as filling the See of Canterbury or York. One miracle
did occur, the elevation of William Temple. There are not likely to
be any others while the Establishment persists. During the present
century, Temple's two-and-a-half years' tenure of the archiepiscopal
See of St Augustine is the only instance (up to early 1961) of anything
like spirituality. While the pronouncements of various popes since
Leo XIII contain a deep awareness of the spiritual problems which

face the modern world, there has come from York or Canterbury all too frequently a note of worldly caution.

Disestablishment is unlikely to come about now as a result of direct pressure from the laity, or from the rank and file of the clergy. If unattainable by frontal attack, it may still be reached by a flanking movement: the reform of the House of Lords. But the danger is that if and when reform of the Lords comes about there will be a powerful movement to enrich with new gifts (this is another smooth phrase employed on these occasions) the ecclesiastical element in the Lords. In other words to bring in the leaders of the Free Churches. Logically, it would be impossible to refuse a place to the Cardinal Archbishop of Westminster, if the head of the Methodist Conference or the Congregational Union came alongside the archbishops and bishops of the Church of England. How, I wonder, would one keep out the Chief Rabbi; or the principal Moslem Imam in Britain, or Mr Christmas Humphreys for that matter, to enrich everyone in the Eightfold Path?

No, the only right course of action is so to reform the Upper House that it ceases to be a House of Lords at all. Of this more later; for the moment I will content myself with saying that the Spiritual Lords should depart therefrom. The Church should have its freedom. The clause of Magna Carta should come true – the Church of England should be free: free to expound the glorious message of the Gospel to every creature in the land. A fighting virile Church with a living message, and an exacting standard of ethics, would do more with five millions of convinced adherents than ever it can with the multitude nominally within its fold.

The present Pope, John XXII, at the Christmas soon after his election, visited a prison in Rome. 'Since you cannot come to me, I must come to you.' Could one of our prelates do the like at Wandsworth or the Scrubs? If not, we shall regretfully have to agree that in some respects Italian Christianity is better. Yet once we English had the *anima naturaliter Christiana*.

CHAPTER NINE

The English Legal System

FROM the prophets, however indistinct their latter-day testimony, to the majestic framework of English law. Here surely we are on firm ground. Here it must be that change is unnecessary, that the Establishment is at its best. We have, it is always claimed, the finest legal system in the world, the envy of all other countries. English justice is as near as we can get to impartiality.

Let it be stated at once that there are immense advantages in the English legal system. One of its features most frequently attacked, the existence of two branches of the legal profession, is indeed a great advantage. In those countries, such as Canada, where a man can be at once both barrister and solicitor, it merely means that a sub-division of labour takes place within a legal firm. Moreover, if the same person does conduct a case right the way through from pre-liminary consultation to High Court hearing, then the lay client never gets the advantage of completely impersonal consideration. In England a solicitor is frequently very much engrossed with a client's case; when it goes before a barrister, the latter is able to be detached because he does not, in many cases, have much (if any) personal contact with the client.

The life of bench and bar together is another very good feature. It is rightly admired by foreign lawyers. The judges are drawn from the ranks of counsel, and consequently are able to appreciate the arguments put forward by both sides.

There is in our law, a great freedom from political pressure. There is not the feeling that a judge can be 'got at' which does occur in some foreign systems. Further, there is a continuous history of English law from the twelfth century, earlier still if we include the dooms of some of the Saxon kings. This is of enormous value. It means that a traditional background of English law is there, with certain principles of the common law running through everything.

Unfortunately, there are less advantageous features. The com-plaints about lawyers' fees, and the law's delays are almost as old as medieval literature. They are aspects of legal work which will be unlikely to be eradicated until the final Assize.

But far more serious than any complaint about costs is the very real obscurity and delay which now afflicts the legal system and for which not the system but, as we shall see, the British legislature is responsible. To understand how this has come about we must go very briefly over the history of English law.

Almost from the earliest times of the growth of English law two systems ran parallel. I am not referring to the existence in feudal England of private justice in the form of barons' courts. These must have been horribly oppressive, until they were at last superseded by royal justice. But as the latter developed, it bifurcated. The king's justices went on circuit and heard the common pleas, and administered the common law. But as the body of positive law grew, so too there arose the necessity of appeals from it. The legal remedies often failed to give justice. A suitor might find that he had gone as far as he could under the law, only to obtain a result which was plainly inequitable. He therefore appealed to the source of justice as of jurisdiction, the Crown. His appeal was for equity as opposed to mere law. The appeal went to the King's Secretary, the Chancellor, the keeper of the royal conscience. The Chancellor acting on behalf of the Crown, heard the appeal and gave what relief seemed equitable. In Roman law one comes upon a somewhat similar viewpoint. When the law failed to give relief, Roman lawyers would sometimes appeal to natural justice. They were at least able to recognise in principle the existence of a natural justice which did not reside in any statute book.

In England a philosophical appeal has never been popular. Hence the Lord Chancellor's jurisdiction came to be known as that of equity, and not of natural justice. Thus two rival systems of law grew up side by side in England, both systems coming under the Crown, but differing in their practice and principles. They were the systems of law and of equity, with the two under separate and, as it can be imagined, mutually jealous judges. Extraordinary as it must seem to a layman, this diarchy in the law persisted until the nineteenth century. During this long course of some 700 years, the jealousies and fears of the two sets of judges broke out more than once in open discord. This was very much the case in the reign of James I. Sir Edward Coke, the Chief Justice of the Common Pleas, came into collision with the Lord Chancellor of the day. Coke gave judgement in some cases, in which the disappointed suitors appealed to the

Chancellor. Coke, ever a choleric judge, gave vent to his indignation
by imprisoning the appellants on grounds of contempt of court.
They were released by the Chancellor. When Francis Bacon became
Chancellor, personal rivalry and animosity between him and Coke
was added to the difficulties and frictions between the two courts.
Finally, James I, who felt that Coke had tended to impugn the royal
prerogative, dismissed him from office. This led Coke to inspire a
campaign on behalf of the common law against the sovereign's
prerogative. Coke died before the outbreak of the Civil War in 1642,
but he had had much to do with providing the parliamentary party
with constitutional ammunition.

During the Commonwealth period, the courts of the royal prerogative suffered a severe eclipse. Some of them, like the High Commission and the Star Chamber were abolished, never to return. But
the principles of equity were bound to prevail, and the Chancery
jurisdiction was revived after the Restoration. Coke had been the
greatest authority on the Common Law. His work, *Coke upon
Littleton* was described as the greatest work of humane science in any
language. Yet although he fought against the Chancellor's jurisdiction, this was too necessary to be overthrown.

It was not until the nineteenth century that the work of reform
begun in the seventeenth century was resumed. During the 150 years
following the Glorious Revolution of 1688–89, there was a remarkable cessation of reform. It could not be said that there was an overplay
of legislation, though many private enclosure acts were passed.
It is a very remarkable fact that during this period (of the later
eighteenth century) several highly gifted writers were of the view that
in Britain a near-perfection had been achieved. Edward Gibbon
summed up his reflections on modern civilisation with the easy
assurance that it could not fall a prey to modern barbarism. This
on the eve of the French Revolution. Similarly William Blackstone in his *Commentaries on the Laws of England* assumed that
our legal system was nearly perfect. At this identical time the laws
were engaging the attention of a very different investigator, Jeremy
Bentham. His life was devoted to reforming our legal system. As the
nineteenth century advanced so did reforms, until at length the
arcanum fidei itself was reached. The sacrilegious idea was put
forward that the legal and equitable systems should be merged. Under
the Appellate Jurisdiction Acts from 1876 the systems were merged.
The Chancellor's Court became the Chancery Division of the new

court. Instead of two Lord Chief Justices, one of the Queen's Bench, the other of the Common Pleas, only one existed under the new system, and he (the Lord Chief Justice of today) was subordinated to the Lord Chancellor. The latter emerged as the undisputed head of the legal system. Moreover, it was decided that in future, in any case of discrepancy between law and equity, the rules of equity would prevail. To this day lawyers are still talking about the equities, as opposed to the law.

However curious it may seem that two systems though merged, should retain some of their separate characteristics, nonetheless a great advance had been won in this union of law and equity. Thereupon it would seem that the forces of reaction began to gather strength. Right up to the 1914 war the law continued to be reformed. Thus the Court of Criminal Appeal was instituted in 1908, giving another chain in the series which interpose between a man condemned to death for murder and the execution of the sentence. In 1911 there was the Parliament Act which effectually and finally removed any real effort at feudalism on the part of the Lords. It really did seem that the law might gradually, in the words of a learned judge, degenerate into common sense.

Then came the deluge. The First World War was the greatest tragedy in the history of this country after the Norman Conquest. As we had not gone through with democracy in the seventeenth or early nineteenth centuries, we did, nevertheless, proceed slowly throughout the period 1832–1914 to enfranchise our manhood. When the war of 1914 broke out we had on the statute book an act to permit of manhood suffrage. The operation of this was deferred to 1918, and at the same time the new women voters (up to the age of thirty) were brought on to the register. All this happened in the period when this country had lost three-quarters of a million dead out of our finest manhood. Then in the matter of expense, whereas before 1914 our total expenditure had not exceeded £200 millions, during the war it had risen to £6,000 millions. It never again sank below the £700–£800 millions mark.

Consequently along with a vast increase in the electorate, and a bleeding off of our best manhood, we experienced a new and vastly enlarged expenditure on all sorts of subjects. The Welfare State was with us. As the Government was required to pay attention to more and more subjects, so the need for greater legislation grew. Large programmes of legislation figured in the offerings of the three main parties. I think it fair to say that the last great example of the sensible codification of laws was the property legislation of 1925. This did something to make the complicated English real property law a little more scientific.

From this time forward there has been a volume of law-making probably unsurpassed in the history of the world. A great deal of this legislation is extremely obscure, and requires continual testing and definition in the courts. It is very often unnecessary. Most people would agree with the principle of Town and Country Planning, namely the reasonable control of development in an overcrowded country. But read the Acts and you will see how little they contribute to such control and how liable they are to promote individual hardship.

I give a practical instance from a provincial city. A woman bought a house for £300. She borrowed the money from her sister who allowed repayment without interest. While £200 of the loan was still unpaid, the house became subject to a clearance order because the road in which it was situated was to be demolished by the local council in pursuance of a slum-clearance drive. Now, under one of the sections of the appropriate Act, compensation could be paid for a well-maintained property. Under another section, compensation was payable on property bought between 1939 and 13 December 1955. The woman's house did not qualify for compensation payment under either of these sections. Be it understood that she was a respectable married woman, both she and her husband were employed, and if her house was not classifiable as a well-maintained property that was the fault of the building. Nonetheless, such as the house was, it suited her and her husband to buy it for their permanent home. To all of which must be added another little touch. Under the Clearance Order, the owner of the house is responsible for its demolition. One afterthought; the land is hers. She can sell it for its market value. Reader, you can imagine the value of a small terrace house in an area being cleared of buildings by the council.

I have told this case in detail because it illustrates the type of problem which is being created by the very laws designed to assist progress. Certainly slums should be cleared. But is it just to deny fair compensation for the little homes which are being knocked down? In all the cases which can be quoted (they appear daily in the press), some law, beneficent no doubt in its framer's intentions, is the agent of rank injustice. The fault is the failure to treat human beings as such. They are units to be manipulated as some impersonal organisers feel is best. There can be no exceptions to the rules.

How does the legal side of the Establishment come into this? It is very nearly powerless. There was a time, not far back, in the history of English law when a great lawyer could be said to know the law. This was true of Coke in the seventeenth century. It was still possible for Blackstone in the eighteenth century. Now it is quite impossible for even the greatest legal brain to know more than a small fraction of current law. Specialisation is the rule in law as in everything else. The late Sir Stafford Cripps was considered outstanding because he was proficient in four branches of the law. It is doubtful if this will again be possible.

We badly need a rest over a five-year period from legislation, while all our laws are overhauled by a committee of leading lawyers. We need the consolidation of many statutes in various branches. We need the revision and in many cases the abolition of much out-of-date or over-running legislation. The fact that one department of Government could schedule Snowdonia as a national park, while another brought it within a hydro-electric scheme, shows the overlapping of many Government measures.

The enormous increase in law-making over the past four or five decades has not opened up great possibilities of litigation. To be healthy and productive of the best legal thinking, litigation needs to be of a personal and private nature, the clash of man with man, of business with business. Since the last war, the State, that Great Leviathan, has stretched out its talons, and seized upon the rights and property of the ordinary citizen. In legal action against Colossus, the citizen can hardly hope for eventual victory. Even if the poor remnants of freedom under law permit such a rebellion against governmental tyranny, it is certain that legislation will be passed to stop up the loophole to liberty.

Thus under the pressure of modern law-making, the legal establishment is suffering. The solicitors are not so hard-pressed, for no matter what may occur, they are still necessary for the purchase of houses, the making of wills, and of contracts, the recovery of debts, etc. But the Bar is under a cloud. In many chambers one comes upon young men, recently called, who hope to make a tolerable living in practice at the Bar. Gradually they realise there is nothing for them and they drift away to various jobs, taking their hard-earned legal knowledge and training with them. No doubt they are very useful in industry and in learned associations, but they must often feel the longing to have practised at the Bar. The Bar is overcrowded. Most people want to avoid litigation so they seldom get beyond a consultation with a barrister. Yet so ingrained is legal habit that many, if not most, barristers would object, on the ground that it was a restrictive covenant, to any measures which might reduce the numbers of barristers in practice.

A fast-growing jungle of legislation, a decline in litigation, and on top of this, the existence of many tribunals over which the courts have no jurisdiction. For with the coming of the Welfare State (Belloc's *Servile State*) has grown a proliferation of bodies which decisively affect the citizen's life. Yet over these tribunals the courts of the realm have frequently no control, since no appeal lies to the latter. In Act after Act, there is a ruling that in the event of an appeal against the Act, such appeal shall lie to the minister of the Government department which is to administer the Act. That a man should not be judge in his own cause has always been a principle of English justice. How can this be upheld when appeal is to be made to a minister against a decision of the civil servants in his own department? Without the least doubt a minister will strive to be fair, but it is in fact very difficult for him to be unbiased.

These several factors combined are responsible for a steady deterioration in the respect paid to law. It appears powerless to aid the citizen in his conflicts with the ever-growing might of the Leviathan so surely foreseen by Thomas Hobbes. It appears all too clearly to be unable to help the citizen in one of the most important parts of his life, his work in a trade union. From a very depressed and humble position some 150 years ago, the trade unions have advanced until they constitute an *imperium in imperio*. The irony of the situation is that their ascent to irresponsible power has been aided by the very law which they now set at naught. It was the immunity given by statute to trade unions against actions for tort, which allowed the unions to build up a powerful position, and to accumulate funds for strikes and the threat of strikes. There was, a few years ago, the famous case of the bummarees who refused to allow a merchant to load his own lorries. He applied to court and obtained an order to permit him to load. The bummarees refused to recognise this. They summed up the position very neatly: We said he shouldn't. He said he would. The judge said he could. He didn't.

All very amusing no doubt, and there are people who prefer to sing and dance at funerals. In this case it is the funeral of English law.

Over-riding all other considerations is the decay of the landed gentry which I described in Chapter Six. They supplied the bulk of the legal talent of the country, but in many cases they can no longer afford to do so. Apart, however, from this they also supplied the sinews of the legal profession in supplying it with its main business. I do not mean merely litigation, although there was a fair amount of this. In the landed gentry class there was always a family solicitor and so it came natural to consult him, and if necessary to use the forms of law. But far more important was the very large volume of business in the form of trusts, settlements and land sales and purchases which were essential parts of the life of the county families. Equally, there just cannot be trusts where there is nothing to form the trust. When out of 3,000 acres, only 300 are left, what prospect is there of making a trust or a settlement?

Despite the failure of the landed gentry, through no fault of their own, and the consequent impoverishment of the legal profession, there still persists the illusion that we are living in a past when a hectoring authority was an attribute of the English judge. Today the manners of Coke are, fortunately, absent from the bench, but too often in giving judgement, especially in the divorce court, there seems to be a tendency to lecture and pass judgement on matters which are not at all necessary to the legal outcome. Surely in assessing and making a judgement the only relevant considerations are legal ones. In one fairly recent divorce suit it was stated that in the final fall out, husband and wife engaged in a bout of fisticuffs. The wife was the bigger and stronger partner and soon rendered the husband unconscious for a couple of minutes. In recounting this story the judge remarked that one admired the man's courage for tackling the lady. On grounds with which this story had nothing or little to do, the wife was granted a divorce against her husband. Why was the story brought in? Without it, the case would never have been noted in the press, but with this addition it became news. A man beating a woman may merit a few column inches, but a woman who can throw her husband over her shoulder or put him out for the count deserves a headline. It hardly seems to come within the dignified viewpoint of the court.

The legal side of the Establishment strives to do its best, but it is trying to cope with an impossible situation. The volume of law imposed upon it by Parliament is so great that it is beyond the skill

of even law tutors to digest everything as it comes along. They have
to resort to specialisation in order to cope.

The reason for the Niagara-like flow of legislation is that the two
main political parties are under the impression that they should
offer at each General Election a fresh programme to the electorate.
What is really needed is a period of administration of the existing
law, with the removal of injustice, the ironing-out of anomalies and
the careful study of what is really needed by the people. The law of
marriage and divorce needs a complete overhaul. It is dominated by
some archaic ideas. Notable among these is the theory that because
two people have gone through a ceremony of marriage, the man is
responsible for keeping the woman throughout life, even when they
part by mutual consent. This idea was completely valid in the days
when a man was the sole bread-winner in a family. It has some validity
now, in cases where the couple have young children or where the
wife is infirm. But large numbers of female divorcees are completely
fit and capable of earning their living. To grant them alimony is a
scandal.

There has been a slight breach in this one-sided aspect of the
divorce laws. A woman can now be ordered by the court to contribute
to the maintainance of a crippled husband. But the urgent require-
ment is not for bits and pieces of legislation but for a proper scientific,
and above all just, recasting of the law. Not only should this apply
to the matrimonial laws but to all other branches of law. New laws
would be made in this process, but large numbers of other statutes
would disappear, and more than anything else, right would be done.

Our law urgently requires to be codified and made clear. It is a sad
reflection upon democracy that codification of law takes place only
in absolute monarchies. Witness the Code Napoleon in France, and
the Institutes of Justinian for Roman Law. But what of the body
through which the ocean of legislation is channelled? For it is not
the legal system which is at fault, but the legislature. In the seventeenth
century great lawyers led the way in reform; today they often protest
in their judgements against the laws which they have to administer.

CHAPTER TEN

The House of Commons

NO study of the Establishment can ignore the House of Commons. The poor, shrinking, self-excusing and unwilling collection of M.P.s – as the Knights of the Shire and the Burgesses of the Town were in the thirteenth century and fourteenth century – have become the dominant power in the State. Once in a session, at the State Opening of Parliament, the Members of the Commons consent to revert, outwardly that is, to their old status. They become the humble apparitors of *toutes les grandes d'Angleterre* (the phrase used in describing Lords Spiritual and Lords Temporal in the fourteenth century), but their self-abasement is only for a couple of hours. The Miracle Play of Westminster is played out to the farce's end, but all the players know that it bears no relation to real life. The Members of the Commons return to their own Chamber to resume the business of ruling the State.

As a matter of historical fact – (within the common knowledge of Macaulay's well-nigh omniscient schoolboy) – the Commons did not reach their position of dominance as the outcome of a natural development. They did, it is true, gradually acquire a position of some importance within 150 years of their origin. A sovereign such as Henry IV (perhaps because of his insecure tenure of the throne) submitted to a considerable control by Parliament. After the Wars of the Roses, however, the Commons as well as the Lords were overshadowed by the Tudor despotism. During most of the Tudor period, the sovereign effectively ruled the country, but there were movements of discontent under Elizabeth I. Even had her successors been much more able persons they would in all probability have had to bow to Parliament. Charles II, who was easily the cleverest of the Stuarts, did so, and it is difficult to believe that any other monarch could have avoided some compliance with Parliament at that time. Moreover, in practice Parliament had come to mean the House of Commons. In the later seventeenth century, in the reign of Charles II, there is the curiously combined phenomenon of assertion of aristocratic exclusiveness in the Lords, with the yielding of control of financial bills to the Commons. It is often said that in the next age the Lords ruled because they controlled, through their cadet relations and their nominees, the House of Commons. Apart from the difficulty of viewing Pitt, Fox or Edmund Burke as nominees, this contention is not borne out by studies such as those of Sir Lewis Namier or Professor Turberville. It was also in the eighteenth century that the Lords began to be recruited from persons rejected from the Commons because of their failure to live up to exacting political standards or in other words these failures as M.P.s were kicked upstairs.

With the Reform Act of 1832, and the gradual growth in the number of voters, the triumph of the Commons was assured. No outside body threatened it. It had reduced the monarchy, severely clipped the powers of the Lords, it did not bother about the Church, so what had it to fear? Strangely enough the troubles came from within its own walls.

Democracy, having come full circle with the complete enfranchisement of every adult male and female at the age of twenty-one, has stultified itself. The electorate is now too big for the M.P. to be answerable to it. If a public-spirited individual takes up a matter with his Member he can be fobbed off, because one vote does not matter any more. The same is true of the small group of public-minded people. An agent will weigh up their voting power and nuisance value and will then inform his Member how much notice he need take of the protest in question, usually very little. But let the movement of opinion be drastic and violent enough, involving sufficiently large numbers, and it is a very different story. Politicians are simultaneously contemptuous of, and terrified by, the electorate they have created. It is to them a Frankenstein, and as Cleopatra said of Octavian, they 'word' the monster. They do not believe that the electors are willing or capable of facing a serious challenge and making a clear-cut decision. They believe that the electorate is interested only in bribes and material benefits. On the face of the evidence from General Elections over the past thirty years, I agree that this is a fair conclusion. Against it, however, can be put the appeal of Winston Churchill in 1940, when he offered to the British people, only blood, tears, toil and sweat, and received a mighty response. True, this was not in an election, but is there valid reason to believe that if the economic position of Britain were put fairly and very clearly to the British people, there would not be a response in peace comparable to that given in war?

Inter arma leges silent, but cannot the measures of total warfare be used, and adapted to our very shifting and precarious economic scene? The method of a clear direct appeal to our people has hardly been attempted in peace time.

Along with this distrust of the people, a distinct welling-up from profound depths of fear, goes what I believe to be a total misconception of the needs of the electorate. An enormous socialising influence is at work, reflected in the successive programmes of legislation proposed by the parties. The theory is that these programmes receive the consent of the electorate at the General Election when they are presented. That is the theory. Now, consider half a dozen items in a typical Government programme. 1. A consolidation and revision of the existing Acts in Town and Country Planning. (A consolidation of some of our jumbled legislation usually results in some clauses of importance being left out, so that a further amending measure has to be passed, after the law on the subject has been 'finally consolidated'.) 2. A bill for the extension of the retirement pension. 3. A measure of financial assistance to a shipping company for the building of a new 'Queen'. 4. An omnibus measure dealing with a number of statutes, and occasioned by, e.g., the departure from the Commonwealth of one of its members, whose citizens then acquire a new status. To be quite fair, this type of Act is usually an *ad hoc* measure, which is introduced during a session rather than before it. 5. A proposal for reviewing the prison system and revising the prison discipline. This may receive some particular publicity but *mirabile dictu* will excite no great indignation, save among the left-wing intellectuals and then because it may not go as far in the soft treatment of criminals as these theorists would like. 6. An agreement with the six Powers of the European Common Market.

It is safe to say that in the heat and battle of General Election a programme such as that sketched out could not be put to the electorate. It would be much more vague and abounding in generalities. Still, in its blurred outlines it is endorsed by the electors. Then it has to be implemented by the Government. At least it is intended to be, but when a party gets down to the actual business of administration, it finds that its preconceived ideas have to be altered or adapted to circumstances. Some measures are eventually carried through from the programme, others are perforce dropped, while unexpected and unforeseen matters have to be substituted. On which the comment should not be that politicians are liars, but that they are so frightened of their electorate that they cannot go to them with a truthful progamme. Conceive an appeal on these lines: Our first task will be to secure the safety of all innocent citizens, and the apprehension, certain punishment, and, if possible, reform of all law-breakers. To this end we shall review our prison system, build more prisons, and codify the criminal law, bringing its penalties into a logical scheme. (At present a father who in a fit of rage blinds his baby goes to prison for six months, a convicted murderer gets a life sentence which means in effect ten years, and a persistent poacher of pheasants can be imprisoned for three months.)

'We shall safeguard the employment of the people of this country by breaking down all monopolies, restrictive practices and out-of-date agreements.' Now a party platform on these lines would not involve much new legislation. Where it did, there would be the compensation that many old and worn-out laws, together with some positively unjust measures, would be repealed. The net result would be a decrease in the legal mass, in the sum total of legislation.

The first duty of a government, we are often reminded, is to govern. The old conception of a government in this country, as in other great civilised states, was that it was the administrative establishment of the land. Its primary duty was to rule, and as for the law, that was administered according to statutes and settled rules, with any amendments made necessary by the passage of time. There was no legislative programme as such, no necessity for the governmental machine to churn out new laws in every session. The universal suffrage of the twentieth century has imbued the political parties with the idea that they must set out things that they are going to do. Hence a kind of rivalry in the production of laws.

It can be admitted that in the more complex society of the twentieth century and in the changed circumstances, more legislation may be needed than in the early years of Queen Victoria.

The idea of minding one's own business, of a man being able to do what he liked with his own, made for appalling cruelties to dependents, whether they were adults, children or animals. The Industrial Revolution made Britain the first manufacturing country in the world; it also transformed the rural economy of Britain into one in which the dark satanic mills mentioned by William Blake were, unfortunately, no poetic hyperbole. The whole history of British industrialism from its early days has been such that bitterness between employers and employed was inevitable. Trade unionism has never shaken off the curse of bitterness, which has given it in its official utterances a political slant in one direction only.

Man's inhumanity to his fellow man is reflected in the horrible slums from which we struggle to free our society. It showed itself in arguments as to the sanctity of free contract, when Parliament discussed the labour in the mines of little children (mites under the age of nine!) and of pregnant women.

To deal with situations of new social and economic problems as created by the Industrial Revolution, fresh legislation had to come. Factory Acts, Education Acts, measures to legalise the association of workmen, all these things were inevitable.

Industrial miseries, by bringing reforms in their train, made possible the awakening of the British conscience to cruelties in other directions. In 1824 the R.S.P.C.A. was founded.*

Its history has now been written by one of its former chief secretaries, Mr A. N. Moss. He has done his best in his early chapters to search out examples of man's care for the other living things which share this world with him. A few cases from the Greek Anthology, the pity of St Anselm, the universal love of St Francis of Assisi, and the humane views of Sir Thomas More – and this is the best even a diligent author can find. Had there been a compilation of the devilries of man and the miseries to the animal world, the twenty-four volumes of the *Encyclopaedia Britannica* would have been insufficient.

Still, at last feeling in England was stirred. The R.S.P.C.A. was formed in 1824; it has done much good work, stopped some cruel sports, and abated others, produced some Acts of Parliament on behalf of animals. It also induced the development of a similar society in America. As a return it was from America that the idea of the N.S.P.C.C. was derived. The secretary of the American S.P.C.A. was asked to intervene on behalf of a little animal which was in suffering. He promised to do so. It was then revealed that the little animal was a small child. The case was actually argued in the American courts on the grounds of the child being an animal, and when the case was won, it was animal welfare inspectors who removed the little human being to safety. An Englishman visiting New York on business heard of this very good association for the Prevention of Cruelty to Children. He brought back to England the idea, and

* A fact which would be amusing if it were not so serious is that the awakening of the British consciousness to the sufferings of children was preceded by concern for cruelty to animals.

ultimately in 1884 the N.S.P.C.C. was founded. It now deals with nearly 40,000 cases a year, of which some 27,000 are of cruelty and/ or neglect. This is not a very good picture of an England which has never had it so good.

I give this digression because it should be made quite plain that many laws which we possess and which were unknown before 1860 are essential to our progress. Laws to regulate hours of labour, to grant recognition of trade associations, to protect children and animals, are with us because in these spheres our consciences, or perhaps it would be better to say the consciences of an enlightened few, have been stirred to action. Such legislation would have been despised as soft and unmanly by our forebears, simply because they were too brutal to know their own cruelty.

Unfortunately, it is not this type of legislation which forms the staple of party political programmes. At least half of the humanitarian reforms of the past 100 years have occurred because of the energetic efforts of private Members of the Commons, tireless reformers who would not be overcome by ridicule or hatred. Government legislation usually takes the form of a vast bumbling. The huge bulk of the Town and Country Planning legislation is a case in point. Again, consider the sphere of company law. No institution is more widespread in the free world than the limited liability company. Without it there could have been only a very much slower development of business operations in the past 150 years. Limited liability is indeed an enormous advance even over partnership. On the other hand, the idea is subject to abuse. To control and prevent abuse is the duty of the law. To this end the law has been revised at several dates. In 1947 there was a Company Act which immediately gave place to a fresh bill, the latter becoming the Company Act of 1948. Here is only one example of wasted effort, to have the 1947 Act, as it were, lying on the table. It now appears that another Act will be required, since loopholes have been found in the law. Meanwhile, no attempt whatsoever is made to deal with the small private company. A person can turn him or herself into a limited company, the avowed object of the operation being to avoid taxation.

Enough has been written to point out the overburdened nature of the political, as of every other side of the Establishment. It is a case, again and again, in every instance, of an Establishment, adequate enough up to the eighteenth or the early nineteenth century, but be- coming more and more strained at the seams with each new development in education, wealth and franchise. Today the Establishment resembles nothing more than a covering which was sufficient for the youth but not for the grown man. In fine weather the outgrown garment looks foolish, but in storms it becomes a serious trouble to the wearer.

What is to happen to the once ample cloak of the Establishment? In the interests of all, it must be re-tailored.

CHAPTER ELEVEN

Antiques versus Utility

THUS far I have traced our titled system through its full length from Crown to gentleman, taking in on the way the peers of the State and those of the Church; the law officers and the Members of the Lower House; always having in mind that behind the actual title-holders stand the large army of the old landed gentry class, now so much in decay. I have noticed the decline, one is almost tempted to call it the fall, of the landed gentry, and the constant effort required to make the Establishment stretch its covers across the ever-widening chasm of the national life. There are, however, many other features of our country's past which will occur to everyone. What of the great livery companies? What of the very large Masonic movement? What of big business, of the armed services, of diplomacy?

Now to examine all these spheres in turn would require a book in itself, devoted to each one of them. They can be touched on, but not gone over in detail, apart from the fact that to handle them properly would need the knowledge of an expert, in each special sphere.

Let us look first at the livery companies. They embody one of the most interesting examples of adaptation in British life. It is not very long ago that they were fulfilling the functions for which they were founded, which was to act as a cross between a trade union and a professional association, combined with a guild having a religious basis, a combination which dated from the Middle Ages. Most of the great livery companies do originate from the close of the Middle Ages at least, and the charters of the greatest were either granted in the fourteenth or fifteenth centuries. But today with a few exceptions they do not fulfil trade functions. Glaziers do not glaze windows, though they do indeed take a great interest in the education of those who wish to become artists in stained glass. They dispense charity. They meet at various times throughout the year in places of great interest and some splendour. It is the same with the other companies. In fact the greater the company the less the likelihood that its members will have any direct connection with the subject matter of the original company. The greatest noblemen in the land tend to be members of, e.g., the drapers, the haberdashers, or the grocers, but they are not, of course, practitioners of those trades. I remember with some glee an occasion in one of the Inns of Court when in conversation with a young man, the son or nephew of a judge, I learned that his family had been for three or four generations, shall we say, glovers. Without thinking I remarked that I was interested in that trade. I shall never forget the lofty manner in which he assured me that his family's connection with the particular company had no association with the trade concerned.

In truth the livery companies are a relic of a feature of European life which has survived to any considerable extent only in England. During medieval times it was possible for a company to be able to control the whole of a trade in a particular country. With the growth of commerce in the later Middle Ages this was no longer possible. As early as the first part of the sixteenth century there were complaints that people were coming into the guilds and livery companies who were not necessarily masters of their craft. An interesting example of this occurred in 1529 with the Goldsmiths' Company when some of those who had actually learned their trade the hard way from apprenticeship onwards, objected to the presence in their company of others who were gold merchants but not acquainted with the mystery of the trade. This objection was not sustained, so it appears, by the courts to which it was brought. In short the livery companies have lived on after the departure of their powers of regulating trades and occupations. The rise of modern capitalism has made the attempt to regulate a trade or business by a company unpractical.

So it has come about that the majority of the great city or livery companies are now composed as to membership of persons of quality as our ancestors would have styled them. Many of the company liverymen are indeed business men, but very few are engaged in any form of retail trade. The livery companies have become another bulwark of the Establishment.*

It may be observed in passing that much the same is true of the great Masonic movement. It has permeated every one of the higher walks of life, and has its grip on very many associations which at first sight would not appear likely to be connected with a quasi-

---

* All those who become freemen of the City of London and liverymen receive a little book, called *Rules for the Conduct of Life*. This book stresses throughout the great need to combine religion with everyday life, and, indeed, points out the necessity of seeking first the Kingdom of God.

religious movement. Masonry is made up on the whole of the upper middle class, with a goodly sprinkling of the aristocracy. The lower classes, if such an expression is still permissible, have to be content with the Oddfellows, the Buffaloes, etc., while one of the more idiotic remarks which one can hear in clubs and meeting places is that 'Rotary is a poor man's Masonry'. It need perhaps hardly be said that rotary has not the remotest connection or resemblance with masonry. There is a certain amount of overlapping between the two movements, in the sense that Masons and Rotarians are often one and the same persons, but there any semblance of a connection begins and ends.

The vast network of clubland is yet another facet of the national life where the members of the Establishment gather together. The desire of most Englishmen who aspire to any social position is to belong to a club, and to the right type of club. It will not do to be member of the Upper Midlingham Sports Club, if one wants to rank on terms of equality with those who are members of Brooks's or the Travellers. No, it must be a club of a certain class, in the West End, and it is surprising how quickly the right type of club is recognised. In addition to the distinctive West End club, there are a number of odd city or semi-suburban clubs which also rank as on the same scale or rather as acceptable by those who do belong to the bigger and more important clubs. These bodies are looked on as awfully jolly 'what, old boy, rather arty, don't you know', and men who are distinguished in the arts or in business but who would not qualify for membership in Boodle's or White's can mix in this other type of club with those who have a common membership in the exclusive West End club.

Livery company, Masonry, clubs, these are some of the marks of a man of affairs. Let me hasten to add that there is nothing stiff about these institutions. They give real pleasure to their members; friendships are made in them which endure for life, and which are solid bonds of character between people who like and respect each other. In all the institutions mentioned, there is stress on character. While the possession of a reasonable modicum of money is essential to participation in the institution's activities, money is not the criterion, and character really does count for a great deal.

The armed forces have for some two centuries supplied the outlets for the more adventurous spirits among the aristocracy and the landed gentry, as well as among those who have come up the hard way from commerce and the professions. The nominal rolls of the army and navy show this to a marked degree; not nearly so much in the R.A.F. Many have made the service their professional career, in many other cases it has been simply the occupation of a few years from the life of a landed gentleman. That side of the armed forces has now practically disappeared. It is improbable that the country or the forces will be the gainer.

The world of business lies strictly outside the sphere of the Establishment as I have tried to describe it; but at the same time it has been, through the centuries, the Establishment's fertile recruiting ground. From moneylender Pole in Edward I's day to Thomas Lipton in the reign of Edward VII, the self-made man has been accepted, warts and all – 'Hang it, the pheasant shooting is good on his estate'; and if some individual of force and cunning has not quite made it, usually his son does. There is, of course, the reverse of this medal – as witness the disastrous occasion when the late Marquess of Winchester, who had been given a business directorship simply because he was titled, was involved in a fraud case.

Thus it can be seen that the tree of Establishment, rather like the tree of Ygdrasil of Norse mythology, spreads its branches far and wide, and its roots permeate the whole of British life. To suggest that it should be ruthlessly purged or pruned, or even cut down, is to wish to alter the character of a country. There are many picturesque ceremonies which are associated with the figures of the Establishment. I would not for one moment wish to remove these. I would even add to them. I do not see why the Master of the Horse should not actually order Her Majesty's horses, and hold her stirrup when she mounts to horse on ceremonial occasions. I would add the heralds of the College of Arms to the retinue of the Sovereign at such times as the Trooping the Colour. I would deepen and heighten such ceremonies. I would revive some of those which have dropped out of use.

But that is a very different thing from saying that I would agree to perpetuating the type of thing which has occurred recently in such instances as the Deanery of Guildford case, or the affair of Wedgwood Benn, or the mess which has been made of the Life Peers Act; to say nothing of the fiddling about with the reform of the House of Lords, or the failure to grasp the nettle of disestablishment for the Church. All these matters indicate one phenomenon and one alone – the refusal to bring the Establishment up to date or to iron out its anomalies. No action is ever taken until it is forced upon the vague 'they' who seem to manage our affairs. Then when they do act, they may be sure to act in the wrong way. At one stage they are all for peers staying as peers – whether they want to or not – as in the Stansgate business; at other times they are altering the fundamental assumptions which belong to the whole idea of a House of Lords – by paying three guineas a day expenses to lords who actually attend. Yet even when a step is made in the right direction, as was undoubtedly the case with payment for peers, it is always taken with too small a stride so that it falls short of what is needed. When something is done which is right, it is usually nullified because it is done for the wrong reason. Pay for peers, yes, but why link it with pay for M.Ps. ? And if it is recognised that peers are no longer automatically rich men, then why not go the whole hog and so reconstruct the Lords that they can be senators who are paid a proper salary? Everywhere we turn there is the spectacle of an Establishment twisting and straining for every inch, and yet never quite stretching to the right limit.

And over everything there hangs the horrible suggestion of what can only be described as a 'done job'. There is this vague phrase, the advisers of the Crown, but who are they? How do they act? We know the results of their action – the man expected to get the job does not get it, and so on, but how do they operate? There is as much secrecy in the action of Establishment operators as if they were engaged on some matter of national security. We are left with the impression that in some unpleasant way all our actions can be rendered useless by the actions of some hidden persons, who are working behind the scenes.

The cases which I have quoted above are merely those which have occurred during the writing of this book.

They can, of course, be paralleled again and again by anyone who likes to look back over his own knowledge of public affairs. They will be balanced in the future, how soon we do not know, by other similar incidents, all of which go to prove one simple truth, that we have an Establishment completely out of touch with the modern life of the nation.

I am sometimes told that I am prejudiced against the aristocracy, and that I am likely to overturn the traditions of England. I well recall, soon after the publication of the first post-war edition of *Burke's Peerage* in 1949, being told by the then head of the Wake family, Major-Gen. Sir Hereward Wake, that he had not expected to find the Editor of *Burke's Peerage* working against the traditions of England. To which my reply was that I did not know that tradition consisted in the maintenance of something which we had come to have reason to think was untrue. This applied then to the legend of the Wake descent from the great Saxon or English patriot, Hereward the Wake. Later, Sir Hereward Wake came to realise that I had no such destructive aims, but was anxious to find out the truth. Indeed, no one, not even he himself, could have wished more fervently than I that the descent from the Wake could have been substantiated. I had always been a lover of Kingsley's romance, *Hereward the Wake*, and I have for years collected the historical notices of the great patriot, who held out to the last against William the Conqueror. Sir Hereward had a sense of humour and before long he sent me a Christmas card with a question mark beside the name Hereward. I for my part inserted a note at the foot of the article in *Burke* in which I gave the sources for the Wake legend and the rival authorities. Even for that little encouragement to the family feeling I was taken to task by some of the severer genealogists in their criticisms.

No, I am not opposed to the maintenance of tradition. In fact I would extend it, but would keep it apart from the business of government. I would remove all mysticism from politics and law, where it has no place, and let it have its proper place in connection with the sentiment of the monarchy and of patriotism.

By this view, I mean that in the spheres which I have surveyed thus far, much that is dear to the sentimental heart should be preserved. I suppose there is no harm and much good in the Westminster mystery play. It ought to be televised with careful explanations, however, so that its invaluable propaedeutic quality should not be lost. The State Opening of Parliament, the Trooping the Colour, are rightly occasions for the outlet of sentiment; the procession of the Knights of the Garter, the ceremonies of the various orders, the Ceremony of the Keys at the Tower of London, all these things are of value in reminding a people of the fact that once upon a time they had greatness, and who knows, may one day stir them to the endeavour again to become great, even though in a totally different manner.

Some years ago, there was a case which, in my submission, was very wrongly handled. This was the application of the Duke of Norfolk to Parliament to have Arundel Castle made, so to speak, his perquisite. It is, of course, his official residence and country seat, but although he is Earl Marshal he receives no allowance for the upkeep of the castle. He wanted to secure this free of rates and charges, in order to provide for himself and his successors an official residence in the proper sense which would serve the Earl Marshal of England. He lost his application, but I think that he should have had it granted to him. He has a leading part to take in the great ceremonies connected with the Crown, and for this task his equipment is financially quite out of date. When his ancestors were made Earls Marshal, they were very rich men, who could afford out of the revenue of their estates to maintain their offices, but now all that is changed. There is no magic in the person of the Earl Marshal which can ward off the effects of Schedule A, and keep away demands for income tax and surtax. The present Duke of Norfolk has had to sell a great deal of his property, since he came of age in 1929. If the State wants him to continue with his work for the country, he should at least have some perquisites attached to the office.

If one looks down the list of the principal officers of state as given in the Table of Precedence it will be found that there are very few offices which are still in action. Most are in commission, like the office of Lord High Admiral; some are shared between families like that of Lord Great Chamberlain. The only untrammelled dignity, which remains in the same family, and which is still discharged in much the same manner as of yore is the office of Earl Marshal.

Why cannot the country afford an Earl Marshal with all the proper trappings? Why cannot we have a good old-fashioned example of what a great nobleman with an hereditary position was really like? There are a great many high-sounding titles still existing in the older nobility. The Earl of Lonsdale is Hereditary Lord High Admiral of the coasts of Westmorland and Cumberland, and Warden of the West Marches. We do not expect him to lead his flotilla out of the little harbours of that rough coast, or take his squadrons of cavalry on patrol of the Scottish border. The Duke of St Albans is the Hereditary Grand Falconer of England, though I doubt if he has ever seen a falcon fly or at least ever set one in flight; he has refused, I hear, to accept the presidency of the British Falconers Club.

So the chances of preserving a great nobleman *in statu quo* are slender. Why not take them? It would be picturesque, it would be useful for educational purposes, and it would be lucrative in the tourist trade.

Not long ago the London Zoo lost its favourite orang-utan, valued at £800. This great anthropoid is found only in the forests of Sumatra and Borneo. It is of the greatest importance to science and humanity that such a creature should be preserved. Every effort should be

made to do this and in view of the nature of modern political development in the area which is the orang's natural habitat, it becomes ever
more important to try to save as many as possible, so that specimens
can be bred in captivity.

Yes, people are willing, and I hope agree rightly to go to great
trouble and expense to keep an orang-utan alive and to preserve his
race. Yet when an effort was made to do something practical to keep
the ancient state of the Earl Marshalship, by giving to the bearer of
the office an official residence, the matter was defeated,

I would like to see a real live great noble of the past preserved in his
native haunts, with servants and retainers, castle and liveries, so that
people might know what life was like in days gone by. I hope that
war will disappear but I would not want the memory of it to be
erased from the collective consciousness, because it would be a bad
thing if this were so. It is similarly advisable that men and women
should know what feudalism meant, and this could easily be done by
keeping up the Earl Marshal's state as it should be without the risk of
having to sell some hundreds of acres here and so many scores there,
to stave off the inevitable end – the day when the Earl Marshal lives
in a semi-detached, and goes out to work on a bicycle.

One can easily find instances of a partial preservation of the
antique. The Duke of Atholl has a small army of 300 Highlanders,
and a very fine sight this is for tourists. It is the only private army in
Britain. Yet there was a time when the existence of retainers was a
terror to the Crown and to all peaceful citizens. Now, so much has
the nobility been tamed of ferocity that a little antiquity of this type
is something to be cherished. Similarly, if the Earl Marshal were to
be preserved in his state as he lived, e.g., at the beginning of the
present century, it would be a good thing, and multitudes of tourists
and visitors would flock to see him and his retinue. It is the only
recognised way of preserving 'big game' whether in the African wild
or in the depths of Sussex. But just as no one in their senses would
wish to see the return of real private armies, so the existence of a great
Officer of State with the old trappings of Victorian aristocracy, does
not mean that we can go on with silly pretences such as the arguments
over Wedgwood Benn, or all the rigmarole to create life peers. I am
in favour of making the pomp and circumstance one thing, and the
reality another.

In fact this is precisely what is done in many departments in
Britain. There is no more colourful or moving ceremony than that

of the Trooping the Colour. I cannot watch it, even on the medium of television, without finding myself moist-eyed. But no one suggests that the army should soldier in scarlet coats and bearskins. The British Army, despite our abdication of empire, is usually on service in more parts of the world than any other national force. Kuwait in 1960, with a temperature of 120 degrees in the shade, made even the wearing of a form of battledress seem ridiculous and cruel. The Trooping the Colour ceremony is only a ceremony, and yet how much more. The centre of the action is a reminder of the days when the Colour of the regiment was carried slowly along the line even in the heat of action so that the soldiers might have a chance to rally. In the modern ceremony the hours of training which go into the skilled performance of the Queen's official birthday are hours far from wasted. They typify meticulous care in the handling of arms, obedience to order, discipline in the best sense – these are qualities with which no worthwhile army can dispense. One has only to compare the Brigade of Guards with the ceremonial troops of the French Republic to see what a proud tradition can achieve. I have discussed with regular army officers what in their opinion would be the effect of putting our army into ceremonial clothes, and not merely having the regiments of the Guards and Household Cavalry in the splendid equipment of peace time. Some have felt that it would be a valuable stimulus to recruiting. One officer may be, I fear, nearer the mark of our degeneracy, for he said that the colourful uniforms of older days would not appeal to young men, not that they would not like the colour or the gaiety, but because such uniforms have to be kept in good order, and this meant trouble.

In everything which surrounds the pomp of the monarchy, there should be tacit or open recognition that a ceremony can well be preserved, for its historicity, or its colour, provided it is not allowed to stand in the way of progress. It is to be regretted that drab clothes and shoddy ways are being permitted to slip into the Court. Lounge suits can be worn at garden parties, and, indeed, the old-fashioned Courts have gone, done away not by popular objection but by what I think is a mistaken idea on the part of some around the throne that they were outmoded. Here, indeed, we have the familiar saying of straining at a gnat and swallowing a camel. The presentation at Her Majesty's Courts, with all the beautiful clothes and ceremonial has gone. This ceremony never did anyone any harm. In fact it was good for trade. But the ridiculous side of the debutante circus has not been abolished. It flourishes mightily, and the newspapers are full of pictures of weird-looking or dough-faced beauties, for all of them are beautiful, according to the society scribes. Yet while this part of our tradition has been quite needlessly removed, some much more important matters are not even touched.

It is in this strange attitude of not touching the essential but of removing the inessential that the frivolity of our present system is seen. What did it matter to anyone except the family and the girl concerned, if she wore her plumes and white dress to the Court? Why do men who go to the garden parties which are a sort of pathetic attempt to cover up the disappearances of the Courts, not wear morning dress? Why is there a tendency in the higher circles to substitute the easy-going dinner jacket for full evening dress?

I think that it is all part of the slovenliness of the present age. An age which delights in sweaters and jeans and weird-looking beards, is not one for the grand occasion.

The same principle of preserving a tradition and a ceremony applies to other spheres.

One of the most important of these is the House of Lords. Whether or not the House of Lords should be reformed certainly on a ceremonial occasion such as the State Opening of Parliament peers should appear in robes and coronets. Take again the heralds of the College of Arms. I would not for a moment deprive them of their functions; there is glamour in their reading of State proclamations such as the one prescribed on the accession of a sovereign, and in their tabards and trumpets. They are another reminder of our glorious past, of the days when knights were bold. *But* the College of Arms is the last great repository of public records to which the public finds difficulty in gaining access. The British Museum Library – one of the world's great storehouses of knowledge – the Public Record Office, and Somerset House, are all open to the public so that their contents can be inspected for a moderate charge, and often for nothing at all. The College of Arms has one of the greatest collections of historical matter which has ever been assembled under one roof, and it is of interest, or would be of interest to multitudes of people, if they were given the chance of looking at the documents, which are held there as in a shrine.

I would not alter one stitch of a herald's tabard, but I would put the records of the College under the care of a staff of civil servants, who would be paid adequate salaries by Whitley Council principles or whatever is the standard, and who would administer the archives at the College with the same dull devotion to duty which is fortunately so much a characteristic of the British civil servant.

Enough of this for the moment. In my next chapter I must endeavour to do justice to this great collection of learning and of medieval precedent, which stands as it has stood for three centuries, in the midst of London's busy traffic, in Queen Victoria Street, hard beneath the shadow of St Paul's.

CHAPTER TWELVE

Abstracts and Chronicles

MOST people have a vague idea of what is meant by heraldry. Chambers's Twentieth Century Dictionary defines the word thus: 'the art or office of a herald: the science of recording genealogies and blazoning coats of arms.' Then, inevitably, a reference follows to the Heralds' College. So heraldry has to do with what the newspapers obstinately persist in calling crests, when they really mean coats of arms. This is no place to give a history of heraldry, but in order to understand the meaning of the College of Arms, which is the U-form, as I think it is proper to say, of the old term Heralds' College, one must have some understanding of the meaning of heraldry.

There are very few states today which have state heralds. The Republic of Ireland has a Chief Herald; Scotland has her own Lord Lyon and a full heraldic establishment; South Africa has a Bill in being to establish a heraldic office, which will regulate coats of arms in the Republic. It is often said that there are state heralds in Switzerland, but on close and recent inquiry I find that this is not so. Sweden has a heraldic office, but though it is of very fine quality it does not exercise as extensive a jurisdiction as our College of Arms. In most European countries, heraldry is a matter of private organisation.

England, in fact, is one of the very few countries to have a wide and deep heraldic connection. Moreover, the administrative body in England, the College of Arms, touches many points of practical importance. Lord Morrison of Lambeth is not the first Commons politician turned peer who has mentioned the prevalence of the wishes of Garter King of Arms. He does have influence on the choice of title by a new peer. The ordering of the great State ceremonials is a matter for the College. Even more so, as we have said, the College has in its keeping a mass of records of great consequence.

How has it happened that this ancient institution has come to exercise so much power in a modern state?

Heraldry is the science of symbols, used first in war, and afterwards in peace. Have there not been symbols of this type from time immemorial in many nations, like the Red Indians of Canada with their

115

totem poles? The answer is that with a few exceptions, some of which are doubtful, the use of hereditary symbols so as to constitute what we mean by heraldry, is found only in two areas – Western Europe and Japan, originating in both in the Middle Ages.

In parenthesis it must be said that some scholars like Sir Anthony Wagner think that there were armorial bearings (another name for coats of arms or heraldic devices) in ancient Athens. In the book of Numbers, there is a reference to the children of Israel being mustered under the devices of their fathers' houses, and the tribes of Israel certainly did have devices emblematical of each of them. But it is anyway certain that the origins of heraldry in England can be found in the increasing use of all-enveloping armour during the twelfth century. At the time of the Norman Conquest, armour was not usually decorated with devices which can be called heraldic. Those who care to study the pictures of the Bayeux Tapestry, in Sir Eric Maclagan's little book, *The Bayeux Tapestry*, will see the shields of the Saxon and Norman warriors usually free from devices. This was in 1066. It appears that this was also the case a generation later when the Western knights went on the first Crusade. Anna Comnena, the daughter of the Greek Emperor, Alexius, says of the Franks (in a very long description) that their shields were bare. It is not until we come to the end of the first half of the twelfth century that we begin to get signs of heraldic designs.*

The probable reason for this is that in the new enveloping armour, which was at first a mixture of plate and mail, one knight fully accoutred was very like another. The only way to distinguish him was to give him some sign on his armour which would enable

* Apart from an enamel or so, the early evidences are from seals, which were appended to documents. Seals have a long history in the story of man's dealing with his fellow man; the great object of the seal is to authenticate a document for the benefit of a person who cannot read it. He must be made to understand that the document comes from someone whose authority he cannot resist, so that as a general rule in such transactions his land or money can be taken from him.

Seals then have this great background of record, far into the past, and so much do they come into the account of early heraldry that some incline to the view that heraldic devices developed from the use of symbols on seals, and thence spread to the armour. It may be so. There was no *Daily Mirror* in the Middle Ages; if a file of it could by some miracle be found for the years 1250-1270 our ideas of history would be considerably altered, for we would then know of much which has passed away. But there was no one to chronicle the early shields and coats of arms. We can only guess at the origins.

him to be picked out by friend and foe alike. Thus came the coat of arms, which took its name from the surcoat (rather like a waistcoat) worn over the armour; the shield, where clearly the new devices would be used; the crest over the helmet; the pennon of the lance which would carry the arms; and the trappings of the horse.

The use of arms spread with great rapidity and, as far as we can judge, with simultaneity over Western Europe. It took in the countries of that area from Norway to Sicily, from Poland to England. Poland is the only Slav country to have a Latin civilisation. Outside Latin Christendom, other races adopted heraldry, but only in imitation. Thus we find it in the Celtic fringe, in the Highlands of Scotland, in Ireland, in Wales; in Russia, but not until quite late, even later in the Balkans; and latest of all in India at the Delhi Durbar of 1911.

But in Japan there is a hereditary symbol called the *mon*, which corresponds to the crest. This has been used for many ages in Japan, and is still the symbol of the greatest families. In Robert Standish's book, *The Three Bamboos*, the title is taken from the *mon* of the Fureno family.

At first in Western Europe, the use of arms was an entirely spontaneous matter. Much controversy has been expended on this subject, but a little thought will soon convince one of the truth of the above statement. There was no one to regulate arms at first starting. Those who wish to go into the intricacies of this matter must consult the various heraldic authorities and armorial writers.* It is enough to give here particulars of a few well-known cases, which illustrate the early history of heraldry. There was a siege in 1301 of a small fortalice on the Scottish border, called Caerlaverock, and in the poem which describes this we hear of disputes over arms. Other examples are given in the famous case of Scrope v. Grosvenor, which is found in two stout volumes edited by Sir Harris Nicholas. In these instances and many others which are known, men are found coming from different parts of England who have the same coat of arms. This proves conclusively (except to bigotry) that arms were self-derived in the early generations.

Nonetheless, it is true that there was need of persons who should understand arms and how to marshal them, i.e., to arrange the wearers

* A. C. Fox-Davies *A Complete Guide to Heraldry* (Nelson) and the same author's *Heraldry Explained* (obtainable secondhand). Also my own books, *The Story of Heraldry* (Country Life, out of print but 3rd edition promised, 1963), and *Teach Yourself Heraldry* (English Universities Press).

in the proper order for a tournament. These men were called heralds. At first they were members of the households of great noblemen and, of course, the greatest man in the realm, the king. In Scotland to this day, there are still three noble families, of one of which the Countess of Erroll is the head, which have their own herald; but then heraldically Scotland is a museum piece of the utmost value.

It thus happened that the King of England's heralds formed part of his household. To this day they remain so, i.e., the Officers of the College of Arms are not civil servants or Government employees in any sort, but members of the Queen's household. In 1407 the King of France altered the arrangement of his coat of arms, so that the lilies as shown before that date are known as France ancient, and since then as France modern. The King of England followed suit, and so it came about that when the French king made his heralds into a closed corporation or college, the English king followed his example. For in the Middle Ages, France was the leader in the fashions of civilised life, just as she has been in modern times in the sphere of clothes.

It was Richard III who, in 1484, made his heralds into a College, so that they would be still part of his household, but have a separate place to live and work in. His endowment shared his fate at Bosworth Field, but the institution of the heralds as a corporate body lived on. In fact it was under the succeeding Tudor kings that the heralds may be said to have attained their greatest influence. After some vicissitudes, they settled down in a building on the site of which their present edifice stands in Queen Victoria Street, with the swirling streams of traffic and the congestion of modern life making doubly attractive the quiet enclave behind the iron-work gates.

In 1529–30 the second Tudor king, Henry VIII, gave the first of the commissions to his heralds, which are known as the Visitations. These were orders to travel in turn through the counties of England and to find out what arms were in use; those which were lawfully borne were to be recorded, and those which were not lawfully in use were to be discontinued. By means of the Visitations the Crown asserted its control over the arms of all its subjects, despite the fact, as I have pointed out, that arms were originally assumed at a man's pleasure.

There are a series of these Visitations, extending right on to the reign of James II (1685–1688). They ceased then owing to the sudden departure from England of that king, and his successors did not care to order strict inquiry into the armorial bearings of their gentle subjects. A natural precaution considering that one of the near successors of James II was a Dutchman, and two others Germans, one of whom could not understand English.

There was another means of controlling arms which was employed by the Crown and that was the Court of Chivalry. This was an ancient court which had existed from the times after the Norman Conquest. It had been held under the Earl Marshal and the High Constable; in fact the latter had been senior. This court was primarily of a military nature concerned with army discipline. It gave rise to the courts martial with which the armed forces are familiar. Arms were part of the paraphernalia of a medieval army, and hence disputes between knights and gentlemen over the possession of arms came under the scrutiny of the court. But as the feudal nature of the army gave way under the Tudors, this side of the court's work fell into disuse. Consequently when the last High Constable, the Duke of Buckingham, became a victim of Cardinal Wolsey, and was executed, the office was not afterwards granted to anyone else, except for a short term, *pro hac vice*. Thus the Earl Marshal was left to continue the sittings of the Court. There was continual criticism of it, and under the troubled times of the early Stuarts, there was strong objection to its jurisdiction. Under the Commonwealth it fell with other courts which were considered as the peculiar instruments of royal tyranny. Unlike courts such as Star Chamber, the Court of Chivalry rose again, after the Restoration in 1660. But its opponents were active, and after 1735 it sat no more until 1954, as I noted in my opening chapter.

In this way the two main weapons for control of arms by the Crown, were lost to it, and for some two and a half centuries, the officers of the College have had to wait for cases to be brought to them.

The revival of the Court of Chivalry in 1954 might seem to have brought back the old jurisdiction. But in effect this is unlikely to happen. Lord Goddard, then Lord Chief Justice, but acting as surrogate or deputy to the Earl Marshal, advised that the movers of the court should obtain an Act of Parliament to re-establish its powers and penalties. Nothing of the sort has been done.

The English College of Arms has, therefore, no effective power of interfering with the use of arms by anyone in England. In theory it has the weapon of the court, but, in fact, this is not likely to be used. Therefore, the original position has been restored, that every man and every institution can use what arms he or it pleases. Until a few years ago, the crest and supporters of the City of London were not registered with the College, though the coat of arms was. This ludicrous position was mentioned in somewhat satirical terms in Fox-Davies's book, *Complete Guide to Heraldry;* Fox-Davies was one of the greatest advocates of the theory that only arms registered with the College of Arms are authentic.

I estimate that there are in England and Wales no less than 50,000 persons or institutions which use arms which have never been recorded. There will be a goodly harvest for the court if and when it is regularly reconstituted under an Act of Parliament.

If – and there we come to the essential nature of the trouble which afflicts the modern Establishment. Either its advocates go too far in upholding an antique form where it has the sanction of law, or they are afraid to get the sanction of law for something which could reasonably claim it. When it comes to forcing Wedgwood Benn to don ermine and viscount's coronet, the law is invoked, although it can be shown that in so doing the law is made to look hopelessly asinine. But when a great modern judge advises the heralds that they ought to get parliamentary sanction for their court which is to control the use of arms, then they recoil from the attempt. Of course, one can feel some sympathy for them, in view of the repulse sustained by their chief, the Earl Marshal, when he sought for the establishment of Arundel Castle as a home for the Earls Marshal of the future.

Let us for the moment look at the more practical aspect of the College of Arms. Whatever may have been its original work, it has come to amass, over four or five centuries, a huge quantity of records. These records vary very greatly in quality. They contain some of the finest work in genealogical research. They contain some of the most amusing statements in genealogical history. All are records, but not all of the same standard. I have known of persons who have indignantly exclaimed that their pedigrees are recorded at the College; only to find that they have indeed been entered there, but on the principle that the material is what the recorder brought along, and that the College does not vouch for it in anyway. On the other hand when a pedigree has gone through the chapter of the College, it receives the *imprimatur,* so to speak of the officials and can be cited as evidence in a court of law. Unfortunately, the College is hindered in its work by the idea of collective responsibility, and by the belief that something is right now if it were declared right in 1667. It is not easy for the College authorities to go back on some of their more ancient brethren, and to say that such and such a recorded pedigree is inaccurate or false. Yet it is known that some of the pedigrees recorded in the College, notably those of some Welsh families, are far from representing historical truth. It would seem better to make a frank avowal of this and to point out that the modern principles, now upheld by all officers at the College, have shown some of the old pedigrees to be false.

Apparently this cannot be done. Why? Here we come again as so often to that strange quality in the Establishment mentality; something which is known to be wrong but must not be put right. What good can result from maintaining in existence something which is recognised as inaccurate or untrue is not clear.

No one would think any the worse of the modern College of Arms if they were to declare that they were not responsible for the behaviour of people like the Tudor heralds. Forgery was well known as a means of clearing up a genealogical hiatus in those times; great men like William Cecil were not above it, any more than Bacon was past allowing his servants to take bribes. Conceptions of morality have changed a great deal since the time of the first Elizabeth. If it were at once frankly conceded that the pedigrees recorded in those days were in need of careful editing before they were used in modern times, it would be better for everyone concerned.

However, that is an internal matter for the heralds. What does matter to the general public is that they have under their lock and key a very fine collection of records which is, as I have said, not readily accessible to the public. The reason given is that they belong to the officers of the Queen's household. But circumstances alter cases, and the huge store of records built up over the past four centuries were never envisaged by the original founder of the College. These records now concern not merely a few titled people, but numbers of persons throughout the world. Wherever there are persons of English or of Welsh descent, the College records are of consequence. They contain particulars of every person in English history who was of importance. They give something about his family. If they could be got at without expense or undue secrecy, the heralds would actually increase the the volume of business which would flow into the College.

What is the procedure now? The inquirer who, as John Galsworthy said, follows the line of every great family and goes to the Heralds' College will be interviewed by a duty officer, one of the junior heralds who goes on duty for two weeks at a time. If the inquiry is then put in, a charge of three guineas will then be made (I believe the initial charge is now five guineas). As like as not, nothing will be found from this research. The reason for this is that there is no central registry or general file at the College.

After this, the inquirer has to decide what he wants to do. He will have guessed that this is going to be not exactly a cheap business. Still, he wants to know. He must solve the mystery of that signet ring, or that old carriage door in the family history. He agrees to a thorough search. For this he pays, what? It varies, depending upon the estimate which can be formed of the work to be done, and the extent of his own means. Obviously it is useless for the best genealogist in the world to examine a case and report hopefully upon it, should the person concerned be unable to find money, the sinews of research. However, we will assume that the inquirer is prepared to put down £50 or thereabouts, and the research begins. It should be noted, in an aside, that from time immemorial the heralds have been able to charge and receive fees. The reason for this is the sufficient one that their salaries, even supposing them to have kept pace with the change in the value of the pound, would be utterly inadequate to enable them to keep going. The total emoluments of the thirteen officers amount together to some £300. So fees are charged.

It may well be that, after some time in research, a well-documented pedigree for some six or seven generations is produced. I am thinking of many cases which I have known, where such has been the result of an inquiry at the College. But the position from first to last is that whatever may be discovered, documents and discoveries, the officer concerned has absolute discretion as to whether to communicate them. The person who seeks information cannot take and handle documents for himself. The records of the College have grown up in the course of ages to form one of the most remarkable and wonderful collections in the whole of Britain. But at the three institutions – the British Museum, Public Record Office, and Somerset House – there are no less remarkable collections, which the visitor is able to handle for himself without a fee or for a very trifling payment. In the instance of Census returns for the year 1861 and later, it is true, Somerset House does not permit access, but this is for the reason, now growing a little thin as regards 1861, that such records may contain details of living persons, who may not want their particulars examined. This apart, the principle is quite different from that which prevails at the College of Arms.

The attitude of the College of Heralds is another example, comparable to those which we have met in the House of Lords and in the higher reaches of the Established Church, which calls for considerable change. It would be perfectly simple for a scheme to be worked out, whereby a body of civil servants – an establishment, as Government draughtsmen love to call it – should take charge of the records at the College. They would control their care and would regulate the hours of opening to the public, the places for seeing the documents, and the degrees of importance to be attached to documents on account of age, just as in the case of the British Museum, where some documents can be seen only in a special room, on account of their age, frailty or rarity. The establishment of such a body of civil servants would not mean any real interference with the original and proper function of the heralds, which is to attend to arms and registration of pedigrees. The accumulation of records and the maintenance of them is a by-product, for which the College of Arms as at present constituted is not adequate.

Yes, it would be easy to devise such a scheme, if it were merely a matter of using one's common sense, but, unfortunately, as in everything else connected with the Establishment, common sense is the last thing to be admitted.

In the College of Arms we deal with a frankly medieval survival. It is worth while taking a glance at the constitution of affairs in Scotland. There the heraldic jurisdiction is under the control of a great official, who was at one time, when Scotland was an independent kingdom, a member of the sovereign's council. This is the Lord Lyon, who is a judge of the Court of Session. He is able to judge a case involving heraldry, etc., in his court, and from his decisions appeal lies only to the House of Lords (in its judicial capacity). Heraldry, moreover, in Scotland, is regulated by the law of the land. Under Scots law (a Statute of 1672) it is necessary for a Scotsman to matriculate his arms in the Lord Lyon's register, or he cannot bear them legally. To use them illegally will involve him in the defence of an action from the Lyon, and there are pains and penalties for any refusal or ignoring of the Lyon's decision. Thus in Scotland, arms are regulated by law, as they should be. It may be objected that this is a continuation of feudalism in modern times, and under the aegis of the law. Very well, grant that it is so. Yet if feudalism is to continue at all, it must come into line with the legal requirements which prevail in the rest of the state. If the Lyon gives a decision which is felt to be unjust, then it behoves those concerned to raise the money to challenge this decision in the House of Lords. In fact there is seldom if ever complaint as to the treatment given by the Lyon. The reason for this is that heraldry being regulated by the law of the land is understood by most of those who would use it. They do not feel that any anachronism or feudal backblow exists in Scotland.

Then again, the Lyon has an Establishment and the officers of this are paid salaries. The fees charged by Lyon Office are all laid down by law, and are much lower than in England and Wales.

In the Republic of Ireland an interesting situation exists as to the institution of a herald. The old usage was for the Ulster King of Arms to control the Ulster Office in Dublin Castle, and to deal with Irish arms and pedigrees. There has always been one amusing facet to Irish heraldry and genealogy. Proof of the use of arms, and proof of a pedigree have always been easier in Ireland than in either England or Scotland. The reason admitted by the Irish themselves, is that the country has been in a disturbed state, and hence it would not be possible to insist on strict proof as in England.

When Mr de Valera really got into his stride, he did not wish to continue with the institution of an officer whose authority came from England and the English Crown. Therefore, after the death in 1943 of Sir Neville Wilkinson, the last Ulster King of Arms to reside in Dublin Castle, he intimated that he would prefer to inaugurate his own heraldic establishment. Accordingly, the office of Ulster was united by the British with the office of Norroy King of Arms, one of the three kings of arms in the College of Arms. This officer now exercises heraldic authority over the six counties of northern Ireland, the Ulster Province. The twenty-six counties of the Republic are left to De Valera's new appointee. Here, at least, is one case in which some common sense has broken in. Furthermore, photostats were taken of the Irish records and lodged in London. However, the Chief Herald of Ireland, as the new officer was called, stepped in to the old Ulster Office, and except that names are changed, he exercises the same control as his predecessor.

We thus have two examples of a sensible usage, one from Scotland, the other from Ireland. The Scottish heraldic set-up allows for full play of the old feudal ideas, but within a framework of the existing law, and with a proper judicial establishment. In Ireland, a new modern heraldic Establishment has been created, which works very reasonably and very efficiently. Answers to queries are quick and charges are low.

In other words in Scotland feudalism in a restricted sense has been established, but in accordance with modern law, while in Ireland, a modern arrangement has been made to deal with the same subject.

Why cannot the same thing occur in England? If people think that the College has little relevance today, they may be surprised to know of the extent of the College's activities. Not only do the officers of the College take a leading part in State ceremonials, and in the devising of titles for peers; but they also are required to prepare fresh coats of arms for modern bodies, such as the nationalised industries, and even for concerns as modern as the Atomic Energy Authority. There are plenty of private individuals who are bitten with the genealogical bug, which leads them to an examination of pedigree, and then of arms. This is not true only of England and Wales, over which the jurisdiction of the College extends. English people or people of English or Welsh descent throughout the world come under the heraldic sway of the College. Nor are they slow to admit this, for quite a large number of persons who live in Canada, Australia, New Zealand, or South Africa, apply to the College for arms. So, too, do many Americans. This last seems curious, for the citizens of a republic which is completely sovereign and independent, to apply to the sovereign of an ancient monarchy, for what is, many say, technically nobility. Thus the behaviour of the College is of importance far outside the shores of England. It would result, not in less business, but in more, if it could be brought about that records were placed under more modern systems of management.

In many ways, the College of Arms represents an entrenchment of feudalism in the very midst of the modern state. If it could be reformed, it would be the key to many other changes which should take place, for it will be found that the College touches upon all the other spheres in which the old medieval England still survives. No peer is likely to get along without some reference to the College. No bishop can hold an ancient see without at some time hearing of the College and its functions, and in all the other branches of the Establishment, the mere gift of a title, whether a knighthood or an esquirehood, brings a man right into the circle of the heralds. Instead of being a backwater, it is the clue to the necessary changes, which will enable us to keep what is picturesque in our old system, while not allowing it to interfere with anything essential, and to reform the Establishment, in order that a new Establishment may be built up to fit the modern age.

CHAPTER THIRTEEN

Lest a More Honourable Man Be Called

THE officers who form the permanent garrison of the ancient
fortress set in the midst of London's commercial roar, bear
picturesque names, which are reminders of more colourful days.
There are three Kings of Arms; Garter, who is the senior, Norroy,
(who now is also responsible for Northern Ireland, and unites the title
of Ulster with his own), and Clarenceux. Norroy means North King,
Nord roy, and has jurisdiction over matters heraldic north of the
Trent, while Clarenceux deals with similar affairs to the south of that
river. Then there are six heralds: Richmond, Chester, York, Lancaster,
Somerset, and Windsor. Below these are the four pursuivants (the
word means 'follower') who are the junior officers. Their names are
Bluemantle, Rouge Dragon, Rouge Croix, and Portcullis.

Reminiscent of medieval times as these fair-sounding titles are,
they are only part of the recording system over which they preside
and which is still in use with a patch here and there after several
centuries. I want now to deal with the subject of the Table or Scale
of Precedence. No one can say that this has not been modernised;
in fact, judged by some of the things so far encountered in this study
of the Establishment, the Table of Precedence is modern. It was
framed first of all in the reign of Henry VIII. It was made at his
express command. This is not surprising for Henry made so many
changes, that he had administered some probably much needed
correctives to the ancient Establishment of his time. His own title
had altered not a little. Not only was he the first king to receive the
style of 'His Majesty' (previous kings had been called 'His Highness'),
he had been Lord of Ireland when he came to the throne. He made
himself King of Ireland. The title 'Defender of the Faith', given to
him by the Pope and subsequently withdrawn, had been regranted
by the simple device of having it entered in with his other titles, by
an Act of his faithful Parliament. Defender of the Faith he remained
to the day of his death, and Defender his successors have stayed.

Henry then determined to have some order brought into the
placing of his lords. Many of the said lords had been removed to

another sphere through his agency, and among the new faces and newer titles, it would be pleasant to know the way, even for the regal memory of so punctilious a king. The most accomplished and high-bred monarch of the time must needs put precedence on a proper footing.

Thus he passed an Act for Placing the Lords, in 1540. This Act is described as a declaratory Act, because it so to speak cleared up a muddle of existing orders and enactments on the subject of precedence. The earliest of these dates from 1339, and the last before the Act just mentioned occurred in the reign of Henry VII.

Nonetheless, although this Act of 1540 has been described as a confirmatory Act, so many changes had taken place in the nobility and constitutions of England, that a new omnibus measure was needed. The greater mitred abbots had gone, with the dissolution of the monasteries; many of the oldest peerages had been made extinct. The great offices of state were beginning to thin out; the office of Lord High Constable had perished (as a permanency) with the last Duke of Buckingham.

This Act was therefore a modern measure. But it is improbable that anyone meant it to last for the next four centuries and beyond. It would have seemed more natural to refurbish the instrument and to bring it up to date in a reign or so. Yet the reverse has happened. Far from bringing out new measures of a comprehensive nature, successive sovereigns have been content to patch and make do.

In reign after reign some change has occurred which has necessitated an amendment to the Table of Precedence, which is based, like the flesh around a backbone, upon the Act of Henry VIII's time. In the reign of James I, there was the invention of a new order, that of the baronets. They had to be placed somewhere, so that an alteration became necessary to the Table. Then under Charles I, there was the second order of baronets, that of Nova Scotia. Various changes were rendered necessary by the successive acts of union between first England and Scotland, and then of Great Britain and Ireland. Some of the most interesting changes have been made in the present century.

It was with some astonishment that many persons learned that the first Minister of the Crown was a person unknown to the constitution, as exemplified in the Roll of Precedence. Yet such was the case until Edward VII, by Royal Warrant, dated 2 December 1905, gave his Prime Minister a high place in the ranks of the greatest in the land.

Until then the Prime Minister had relied either on good breeding and common sense for his position at functions, or else on some extraneous rank which he possessed independently of his status as Prime Minister. So many of the eighteenth-century Premiers had been peers, that their rank would by itself have given them a place in the Table.

The various orders of chivalry which have been created in the last 100 years have been placed in their appropriate places in the list: orders such as the Star of India, the British Empire, and St Michael and St George. Then there are places given to the judges and other legal functionaries, mostly following upon the legislation which united the two branches of English law, common law and equity. In the present century some special enactments have been necessary, beside that which related to the Prime Minister. There was the case of the High Commissioners in London for the Commonwealth. Technically they do not form part of the Diplomatic Corps but they enjoy the same precedence as Ambassadors. Enjoy is incidentally the proper word to use in this context, though I have often wondered how much anyone on this or any other list of Precedence enjoys his or her position. However, the High Commissioners now rank after the Lord Privy Seal, a very considerable height in the more elevated regions of the topmost people. Then again a visiting Cabinet Minister, from one of the Commonwealth lands, is given precedence with, but above, the High Commissioner of his country. Prime Ministers, from these lands, however, rank immediately below the Premier of the United Kingdom.

The position of the Duke of Edinburgh has been regulated by royal warrant of 22 December 1952, so that when he is with the Queen, he takes precedence immediately after her.

The latest addition to the list is the royal warrant of 24 July 1958, where the position of children of 'any Lord of Appeal, or any such Life Peer . . . or any Life Peeress created in exercise of the powers aforesaid' is defined to the intent that they may 'enjoy on all occasions the same style and title as the children of Hereditary Barons . . . with rank and precedence among the children of Hereditary Barons in accordance with the date of the appointment of their father . . . or of their mother as a life peeress respectively.' This is the ridiculous regulation which bestows upon the children of life peers and peeresses the style of Honourable.

So here we have a much-amended measure, as one might expect

over a period of 420 years. Still, perhaps it could be averred that this was a means of saving trouble, and avoiding the expense of promoting an Act, etc. But leaving such fantastic ideas out of the account, the list, even without the patchings, is hopelessly out of touch with reality. The Lord Mayor of London does not appear in it. There is, as one might expect, no place for the Cardinal Archbishop of Westminster. There were no longer any cardinals when Henry VIII had occasion for the Act. Things are adjusted differently now and I well recall one instance when the Cardinal of Westminster was to dine at an Inns of Court, and the question arose, what was to be his position? On this and many other occasions, the List does not give any guidance, but it continues to give guidance on the position of persons or classes who either do not any longer exist or whose importance in the real scale of rank has altered very greatly. Few men are higher in importance in government than the Chancellor of the Exchequer, yet he is separated from his chief, the Prime Minister, by a wide expanse of nobility, even coming behind the eldest sons of barons. In short, just as with the Westminster Miracle Play mentioned earlier, the official Roll or Scale of Precedence gives us a picture of what things were like in the realm some three or four centuries ago. While the position of the Prime Minister has been catered for, and also that of the High Commissioners of the Commonwealth countries, on the whole the framework remains of the scale of rank and order of precedence which was deemed fitting in the times of the Tudors and Stuarts. The Scale is a most valuable guide to the idea of the Establishment, which as I have had occasion to point out is really a frame dating from past centuries stretched across the body of a modern state.

It is worth analysing this Scale in some detail. No one will grumble at the arrangements set out for the Royal Family. The Royal Family are par excellence the family set apart, and as we have seen, set even more distantly from their people since they parted with executive power and became lay figures rather resembling a *deus ex machina* of the ancient drama. Then after the royal house come four eminent personages; these are the Archbishop of Canterbury, the Lord High Chancellor, the Archbishop of York, and the Prime Minister.

I would submit that this order of importance is not necessarily in touch with the realities of modern life. There can be no doubt that the Archbishop of Canterbury was, certainly until the time of the compilation of this Table, the most important subject in the realm.

E

In strict theory he should still be so, but is he? Does it occur to the ordinary man or woman that the Archbishop is the leading man after the royal house? If he were, then this country would be in a better condition, for it would recognise the spiritual basis of true civilisation, and we should not now be overwhelmed with materialism. But in fact this is not so, and while the vindication of the spiritual realities which lie behind temporal things is the duty of the Archbishop above all other ministers of religion, it is not seen as his principal task by the multitude.

When we come to the office of Lord Chancellor, we have one of very great dignity and importance; he is the head of the legal system of this country. But when the Table was made, he was also the keeper of the sovereign's conscience, and his principal minister. With the decay in the royal power, the power of the Chancellor waned, and today no one would look for a strong political pronouncement coming from him. It may be that in the remote periods of the Middle Ages the Chancellor did deign to notice a clerk who worked in the Exchequer; today that clerk is the powerful Chancellor of the Exchequer, whose policy can make or mar the success of his party's fortunes in the General Elections, and who is responsible for the financial guidance of his country. Together with the Foreign Secretary, the Chancellor is among the three most important men in any government. We shall not find the Foreign Secretary anywhere in the Scale as such; he has to assume the disguise of a Privy Counsellor in order to merit a mention. True, it is unlikely that a man would become Foreign Secretary without having received the honour of a Counsellorship, but it seems strange at least that no mention of his position should be given.

From these four high personages, we pass to some anciently important offices mingled with some which are of continuing or even enhanced importance. The Lord High Treasurer; Lord President of the Privy Council; Speaker of the House of Commons; Lord Privy Seal; High Commissioners in London; Lord Great Chamberlain; Lord High Constable; Earl Marshal; Lord High Admiral; Lord Steward of Her Majesty's Household, and Lord Chamberlain of the same, and Master of the Horse. Now out of this list two offices are the product of changes, as to their inclusion, made necessary by modern times. The Speaker owes his high precedence to an Order in Council of 30 May 1919. The High Commissioners I have already mentioned. Three of the other offices are not now conferred, except in one case for a very short period – High Treasurer, High Constable, and Lord High Admiral. The last is in commission and has been for some considerable time. The Constable's post is filled *pro hac vice* during the Coronation. The Constable was the senior colleague of the Earl Marshal, but fell in the reign of Henry VIII. The Lord President and Lord Privy Seal are high offices for leading politicians, often, in the case of the Privy Seal, when some tasks to which it is not easy to assign a ministerial title have to be carried out.

After these great offices of state, we come to a portion of the Scale which occupies nearly half of the whole. This is concerned with the peers, from Dukes of England down to Barons of the United Kingdom. It may interest those who are not completely *au fait* with the intricacies of the nobility to know that as there are five orders of nobility, there are also five classes within each order. Thus we begin with the Dukes of England, and pass through the lesser gradations of Dukes of Scotland, Dukes of Great Britain, Dukes of Ireland, and Dukes of the United Kingdom and Dukes of Ireland created since the Union of Great Britain and Ireland in 1801 to form the United Kingdom.

The reason for these ranks within the supreme noble rank of duke, is derived from our national history. At the union of England and Scotland in 1707, the peers of England were given precedence, because of the greater importance of the country; dukes created after 1707 would be of Great Britain and there would also be Dukes of Ireland, with Great Britain for obvious reasons taking precedence over that country. After 1801 we have Dukes of the United Kingdom and of Ireland created after the Union. Exactly the same pattern is repeated for marquesses, earls, viscounts and barons. Between the groups of nobility are interspersed various categories of the sons of peers. Thus the eldest sons of Dukes of the Blood Royal come after Dukes of Ireland created since the Union. Dukes' eldest sons come after the Marquesses of Ireland created since the Union. After Earls of Ireland, etc., come a little group, consisting of (and in that order) younger sons of the Dukes of the Blood Royal, marquesses' eldest sons and dukes' younger sons. In this way we gradually work our way down the Scale until we reach the younger sons of barons. The Bishops of the Established Church come between marquesses' younger sons and the Barons of England. There is also a place immediately after the bishops, where a single line gives hope of place to the Secretaries of State if of the degree of a Baron. This would have accommodated numerous politicians of the seventeenth and eighteenth centuries when peers often held high office in the State.

In this part of the Scale we have the reflection of the ancient idea that the magnates of the realm are the most important people in it, and that those magnates are largely peers. For not only do the peers have a great place in the Scale, but they would until the nineteenth century have filled most of the offices which I have listed above, as coming between the Prime Minister and the first wearer of a ducal coronet. Thus the Scale is built yet on the ancient idea of peers, as wealthy men and men of public affairs, an idea true enough at one time, but no longer true. Can anyone think of many of the peers, whose exploits in matrimony, debt and dishonour are so frequently chronicled by our newspapers, really taking up the high posts of modern government?

After the lowest rank in the peerage (Baron) has been given his due place, we come upon some officers of the royal household; then to Secretaries of State, who are below the degree of a baron. This would, it is true, take in the Foreign Secretary and the Home Secretary, but surely such high personages should have their own place, by the name of their official title? After barons' eldest sons, we have the knights of the three principal orders of chivalry followed by Privy Counsellors, Chancellor of the Exchequer, Chancellor of the Duchy of Lancaster; then comes the Lord Chief Justice, the Master of the Rolls, the President of the Probate, Divorce and Admiralty Division of the High Court. This last entry derives from the Administration of Justice Act, 1920. After this come the Lords Justices of Appeal, under various Acts of Parliament, and then the Judges of the High Court. We then revert to viscounts' younger sons, etc. Finally, when the least of the scions of nobility has been well and truly handled, comes what may be termed the depressed class among the aristocracy. These are the baronets, and I have already explained some of the curiosities of their position. To the question, what is a baronet? the easiest answer is, a species of hereditary knight, but this reply is as repugnant to the baronets themselves as to the pundits of peerage. Personally, I do not believe that the title of baronet as used in the Middle Ages, a few instances of which can be gleaned from the industry of the late Mr 'A Briton' in his *The Baronetage Under Twenty-Seven Sovereigns*, was anything more than a corruption of spelling for the term 'banneret'. Be that as it may, the position of the baronets in the Scale is fixed by letters patent of the reign of James I, in the ninth, tenth and fourteenth years of his reign. In many ways the position of a baronet is the most enjoyable in the whole range of our titles, for he has no tiresome necessity to serve in the Lords; he can serve, if he wishes and is elected, in the Commons, and on the other hand can go around the world without any qualms at all, making any Joan a lady, and when he dies, his son, if a Member of the House of Commons, can quietly succeed to his title without any fuss about a by-election. However, by now the reader may have gathered an impression that I do not expect to see any glimmerings of common sense in the matter of titles. If we must have hereditary honours, why not baronets only, as no one would then be disturbed at all?

From the baronets, who are never clearly classed with the nobility, though they do possess hereditary honours, we come in the Scale to a collection of the knights. The three great orders have already been placed, and now it is the turn of the Knights Grand Cross of six other orders. After them come the Knights Commander; finally, the Knights Bachelor. Thus, the original order of knights is put at the very end of the table of knighthoods although it is from this ancient and pristine model that all the others have branched off. Even the Garter is only a Mark I so to speak of the prototype of chivalrous distinctions.

Wedged in between the Knights and the Companions of the various orders come three legal classes. They are the Official Referees of the Supreme Court; Judges of County Courts and Judges of City of London Court; and Masters in Lunacy. Incidentally, in passing, what a delicious title is the last. One can almost hear the sarcasm. 'What's your job, old man?' 'Master in Lunacy'. 'I never doubted it, old man.'

Following the last of the legal luminaries, come the Companions of seven orders, the last being the Distinguished Service Order. Then come a collection of classes, which ought to be reproduced here, if only to show the meticulous care with which the Scale can be handled, once authority has a mind to do so. Here we have:

Members of the Fourth Class of the Royal Victorian Order.
Officers of the Order of the British Empire.
Companions of the Imperial Service Order.
Eldest sons of the younger sons of peers (the bright effulgence
    of aristocracy is a little dimmed at this remove).
Baronets' eldest sons.

Eldest sons of the Knights of the Garter.
Eldest sons of knights, according to their fathers' precedence.
Members of the Fifth Class of the Royal Victorian Order.
Members of the Order of the British Empire.
Baronets' younger sons.
Knights' younger sons.
Esquires.
Gentlemen.

Here again in the last few classes we encounter that complete lack of realism which is characteristic of the Scale. For consider that an esquire may be a very distinguished surgeon or Q.C. or the greatest living architect (there have been cases when such a person received no other honour than arose from his own professional eminence, probably because he was too outspoken), and that such a man may not be classed in the Scale except behind a mere nincompoop, or even a wastrel, who has done nothing with his life except to be born the younger son of a baronet or knight. In any event I am wrong to assume that my eminent lawyer or surgeon or architect is necessarily an esquire. For when after the war I had occasion to revise the printed version of the Scale in *Burke's Peerage*, I referred the matter to the College of Arms. Among many interesting conclusions which were drawn, there was one concerning esquires. It appears that not until the seventeenth century did the lawyers begin to insinuate themselves into the rank of the esquires, or perhaps we could express the operation more popularly by saying that they muscled in. They wrote themselves esquires. In this country something which occurred in the seventeenth century is of yesterday. It has not necessarily incorporated itself into the feudal system of England. So my advisers looked with a somewhat jaundiced eye upon the legal gentlemen who had become esquires. As to doctors they just would not hear of them. So our doctor, however distinguished for medical skill and attainments, cannot expect to breach the Castle Dangerous of titled privilege. He must be like the peris in the old Arabian fable, forever outside that heaven of honour, the Scale of Precedence, and gazing wistfully within the paradise which he may not enter. As a matter of fact any distinguished doctor who wants titled honours should consult a psychiatrist; in his skill with the body, he has obviously neglected the care of the mind.

There then we have the official chart of the ocean of title and honours, the guide to all the little ribbons and medallions which glimmer and glitter at City banquets and state functions. It is not an unskilful document. Indeed, great care has gone into the preservation and steady extension over 400 years of the original rough draft of Bluff King Hal. But it is a care which is directed to the maintenance of something which has never been a reality at any time since the upheaval of the seventeenth century.

The true Scale of importance today lies in achievement. The holders of some Government offices are now of vastly greater influence than those who come above them in the official scale; similarly there are many very influential persons who are left out. I agree that it would not be easy to put in a class labelled, tycoon, eldest sons of tycoons, younger sons of the same, etc. But it would be perfectly simple to recognise achievement in industry by making some official class which would give to the real leaders of our country their proper place.

In truth, the official Scale is the summing up of the cloying and cluttering feudalism of England. It so happens in the course of writing this book that I have collected instance after instance within the space of a few months of the fetters of the feudal past, which still cling to the limbs of the British people. Among them are the injustices done in the name of an archaic honours system. It may be thought that they are of small consequence, that greater matters require our care. Yet small things have their profound influence, and are apt to be the grit which holds up the intricate machinery.

Furthermore, under the guise of keeping up our traditions, we are in danger of preserving rubbish from the past, which no longer has, even if it were conceded that it ever had, any value in the morale-making which is absolutely vital to a great nation; especially a nation in our position when we are coming to the crisis of our fate.

CHAPTER FOURTEEN

The Feudal Fetters

ENGLAND is still bound, like some ancient building, by the ivy of the feudal ages. In the eighteenth century an old ruin, of some castle or abbey, was little esteemed unless it were mantled o'er with all corroding ivy. It was not until a true school of archaeologists and historians arose who wanted to preserve the worthwhile monuments of the past, that the task of cleansing the noxious plant, and others of like nature from the buildings of the Middle Ages, became a matter of urgency. It could be that a similar task awaits the modern generation. To take another simile, I have often found in my investigations of pedigree that beneath some ridiculous legend there is concealed a really worthwhile ancestry. In the cases both of the building and of the pedigree, only a resolute effort to remove the rubbish and encumbrance of the past can enable us to see the noble proportions so long concealed. To this may be added the fact that in several fields the perpetuation of things which have long outlived their usefulness, is actually retarding our necessary progress. Not tradition, but the misuse of tradition is the foe.

In the course of writing this book, I have been given so many examples of the cloying and retarding influence of things ancient which have been preserved solely through mental inertia, that I am more likely to be accused of offering too much rather than too little. Some of these cases I have touched on lightly, but now wish to deal with them more thoroughly. Others have been handed to me on a plate by the intransigence of the mysterious 'they' who rule the Establishment.

Among those I have not previously discussed comes the instance of the second barony which has been conferred upon Lord Fairhaven. The present peer was so created because it had been intended to confer a barony upon his father, Urban Hanlon Broughton, M.P. for Preston, who died in 1929 before his intended elevation. His elder son was then created the first baron in his father's stead with the style and title of Baron Fairhaven of Lode, in the County of Cambridge. His younger brother Henry was given the rank of a baron's younger son, which would have been his had the father lived to become Lord Fairhaven. But the letters patent limited the descent of the barony to the heirs male of Lord Fairhaven lawfully begotten. Now the first and present Lord Fairhaven has no children and the barony would, therefore, normally become extinct with the peer's death. However, this is not to be, for in the *London Gazette* for 25 July 1961, there was an announcement that the Queen had been pleased to create Lord Fairhaven a baron twice over. He has become Lord Fairhaven of Anglesey Abbey, in the county of Cambridge. This second barony will have a special remainder, as it is termed, which can enable it to pass to the recipient's brother. Thus the Hon. Henry Rogers Broughton will become the second Lord Fairhaven if he outlives his brother, or else the honour will pass to Henry's son, now a man of twenty-five.

Into the intricacies of this most interesting double creation it is not my purpose to enter. I am only concerned with one thing, which is that it was found necessary to issue two letters patent. The original letters patent which created the barony of Fairhaven could not be changed. They had passed the Great Seal, and no change could be permitted. Therefore, Lord Fairhaven has to have a dual personality, he is both Lord Fairhaven of Lode and Lord Fairhaven of Anglesey Abbey. A *reductio ad absurdum*, for surely the Fountain of Honour can turn the stream of honour in another direction without being bound and confined by the acts of her predecessors? It is all reminiscent of the law of the Medes and Persians, in the Book of Daniel, 'which altereth not'. So because of this unbending law, poor Daniel had to be thrown to the lions, although the King who had made the law did not want to kill Daniel yet felt himself bound not to alter his own laws. It may be argued that in the present British case, no serious result will ensue. The operation of this 'law', or rather customary absurdity, will always be confined to a few persons, of noble lineage or at least noble title (not always the same thing). Can we be so sure? Once upon a time, in 1931, England was governed not by Parliament but by Order in Council, during the financial crisis, when Parliament was dissolved, and some pretty drastic regulations came through by Order in Council. Can we be so certain that a measure will not pass the Great Seal of vast importance to the majority of citizens, and which may create some wrong or grievous anomaly, which we shall be told cannot be altered because it has passed under the Great Seal. This type of excuse is often a wonderful way to hold up a reform.

Turning to the more ludicrous side of the matter, we can recall instances in which an absurdity did pass the Seal, and could not subsequently be altered. It often seems curious to the simple that the head of the house of Cavendish, the Duke of Devonshire, should have no strip of land in Devonshire, but all in Derbyshire. It is said that the title as set out in the letters patent should have been Derbyshire, but was altered to Devonshire by a mistake. No change possible. Other cases of a similar nature exist. It is tempting to reflect what might have been the case had one of the old sovereigns of England – when they were still sovereign and could afford to indulge in human behaviour – ennobled one of the animals in the old menagerie which was kept for so long in the Tower of London. After all, the Roman Emperor Caligula made his horse a consul. He was supposed to be mad, but the action may have been dictated by a contempt for the Roman senate. Suppose under the Tudors or Stuarts an ape had been made a lord *à la* Caligula, and letters patent had passed the Great Seal, would there have been a cancellation when the regal mind reasserted itself, or would the noble simian's descendants still be ranked among the peers, like the Roman horse among the *fasti consulares*. It is a fascinating thought.

Then there was the Guildford Deanery case when we were treated to the by now famous remark of Archbishop Fisher: 'It is no criticism whatsoever of Mr Boulton's ministry that the Crown's advisers should have come to the conclusion that they must look elsewhere for a Dean. I know that for some time they have been engaged in their usual careful inquiries and consultations.'

This in a letter to *The Times*, and a reader commented (10 May 1961), 'In view of the importance of this matter and of the questions of principle which it raises may we be told: – (a) Who are the Crown's advisers and (b) the nature of their usual careful inquiries and consultations.'

Well, who are they? We are never likely to know. Despite all the apparatus for publicity which exists today and which some people find it so hard to elude, no one can tell us who are the Crown's Church advisers. The most that the most indefatigable newshound can produce is that various persons go to see the Patronage Secretary. But who those persons are or what their mission, no one has said. It resembles that wonderfully well kept secret, who was the author of the celebrated Preface which appears each year in *Crockford's Clerical Directory?* I say 'was' because the authorship has been attributed to more than one ecclesiastic who is now dead. Yet the

Preface goes on with its often sneering comments on ecclesiastical affairs so that there must be succession in the authorship.

Nothing that I can say about the Guildford case can equal the condemnation pronounced by one of the Church's own Proctors in Convocation. The Rev. J. C. Wansey was reported in *The Times* and in the *Daily Telegraph* (3 July 1961) as saying in a sermon in Guildford Parish Church, 'At a time when new life is surging through the veins of the Church of England, safe men are being appointed as bishops and fire extinguishers as deans. Today, when a man is appointed bishop, he goes not into the van of the Church's life, but as it were, into the guard's van, where the brakes are. How different from the early Church.'

Yes, very different. The Church which counted Cyprian among its martyrs, prevailed over the world because it did not agree with the world. Whatever may be said about medieval popes or renaissance pontiffs, the first thirty Bishops of Rome have M for martyr beside their names. Constantine would never have adopted Christianity as the state religion if it had been the weak flabby thing which it often is under the tyranny of the British State. Or rather, I should have said, under the meddling of the Crown's advisers, those unknown and all-powerful persons.

It should not be thought that the evil of the present system is passing without rebuke or comment from churchmen. In the Convocation of Canterbury, a group of proctors of the clergy were unable to place on the agenda any reference to the matter concerned, about the Guildford appointment. 'A proctor who rose to mention that the Lower House had lost one of her most respected members by the strange turn of events was told to sit down'. (*Times*, 9 May 1961.) This sounds very like totalitarianism. The Bishop of Southwell also made the comment that 'nobody outside the inner circle knows how appointments really are made.' 'Who advises the Prime Minister?' he added. (*Times*, 30 June 1962.)

Nor has the matter of Church appointments ended at Guildford. The subject of the election of bishops has come very much into the picture. On 12 August 1961 at the election of the Bishop of Peterborough as Bishop of London, Canon Collins, Precentor of St Paul's Cathedral, voted against him, in protest both over the new bishop's views on nuclear arms and over the election process as a 'farce, a relic of bygone days'. (*Daily Telegraph*, 14 August 1961.) The system against which Canon Collins protested can be best explained in the following words from the *Encyclopaedia Britannica*, which in cold matter-of-factness tell all that is necessary: 'According to the provisions of this statute, upon the avoidance of any episcopal see, the dean and chapter of the cathedral church are to certify the vacancy of the see to the Crown, and to pray that they may be allowed to proceed to a new election. The Crown thereupon grants to the dean and chapter its licence under the great seal to elect a new bishop, accompanied by a letter missive containing the name of the person whom the dean and chapter are to elect. The dean and chapter are thereupon bound to elect the person so named by the Crown within twelve days.' (Under the article, *conge d'élire*, 1938 edition.)

There have been no refusals since the Reformation. The farce has been gone through. At one time it was a blasphemous farce, since prayer was offered to God for His guidance in choosing one whose name was already known. I believe that I am right in saying that this particular piece of offensiveness has now been done away, but it is still most repugnant to all good feeling that anyone should be called on to go through the farce of electing one whom they know they must elect. There is also the ever-abiding consideration that the person who is to be elected may not, in the honest opinion of the electing body, be suitable. He may not be suitable for the office proposed, not only in the minds of the chapter, but of the general Church public.

Why cannot a relic of this nature be swept away? Yet even if the obdurate hardness of tradition could be removed, there would still remain the fact that the major appointments in the Church of England are made by some mysterious agency, referred to as the advisers to the Crown, whom only a tiny minority can know. In days gone by, the Crown did actually appoint, and when the nation was composed of members of the Church of England, with the sovereign as that Church's chief layman, there was something to be said for the system. It could always be argued that a great agency for influencing the nation must be to some extent under the control of the Crown. But now that the transfer of royal power to the Government of the day has taken place, the Crown no longer appoints, save in a nominal sense. It follows, therefore, that the Prime Minister must make the choice, and he may well not be a member of the Anglican Church, or even a Christian. Furthermore, it is too much to expect that a Premier, burdened with the cares of modern office, can really be able to pick and decide upon the most suitable bishop or dean. He must be advised, but how can the Patronage Secretary know the needs of the Church? But then he is advised by the advisers to the Crown. Who are they, and by what authority do they speak for us all?

This is the impasse, and as the cleavage between the Church and the nation grows ever greater, this matter of the selection of the Church's chief pastors becomes ever more important. Listen to this: 'Archbishop Outpointed. In England mop-haired Adam Faith, 21, the current king of rock ... last week argued religion for half an hour on BBC-TV with the Most Rev. Frederick Donald Coggan, Archbishop of York. Faith proved rather more than the Archbishop had bargained for.' This is a perfectly justified remark taken from *Time* (9 Feb. 1962). I watched the interview and can only say that in my view the Archbishop was outpointed almost every time. A wonderful opportunity was given to him to set out Christianity to youth – and he missed it. I agree with the final comment in *Time*. 'The encounter between cocky, yet questing youth and churchly authority caught unawares did much to explain why, among more than 27 million Englishmen baptised as Anglicans, fewer than 3,000,000 are registered as active churchgoers.' I could not help contrasting this ineffective and (on the Archbishop's part) timorous interview with one which I saw some years ago on television between a number of young journalists and Fr Agnellus Andrew. It was quite impossible for the journalists to get inside his armour, and he remained the winner.

I am afraid that the sort of weak discourse and ineffective presentation which is at present characteristic of the Church's leaders cannot cease until there is a definite change in their mode of appointment. Until a system is brought in which gives the Church the right to elect its own leaders we shall perpetuate the 'safe' leadership which is steadily driving a wedge of misunderstanding between the mass of the people and the Church. The present leaders don't seem to realise that their trade is, frankly priestcraft – the craft or trade of a priest. Never do Catholics forget the position of their priests, who are professionals from beginning to end; why cannot other religious bodies emulate them? I know only one Church from within, the Church of England; it is the system of appointment within the Establishment which gives us the wrong leaders who can be relied on to muff their chances when they do occasionally venture on debate with modern folk.

We now come to something already mentioned which cannot anyway fail to be known to everyone in the country – the Stansgate affair. In its later stages this controversy exactly illustrates the manner in which the chains of the past still grip the British people. In the by-election held in May in Bristol, S.E., the two candidates were Benn (Stansgate) and Malcolm Sinclair. The latter, the Conservative candidate, took every care to inform his opponent and the electorate that votes for Benn were thrown away. Nonetheless the electors of the very independent city of Bristol voted overwhelmingly for Benn. His majority, which had been gradually sinking at General Elections over the last few years, now shot up to a figure of 13,000. He had 23,000 votes, and Sinclair 10,000. There is here a curious loophole in the law, because Benn had been allowed by the returning officer to stand, and his election was also declared by the returning officer. Yet he was denied admittance to the House of Commons. Then on top of that his Conservative opponent, as he had promised, brought forward a petition to have his election set aside, and himself declared M.P. for the division. This petition was duly brought and presented to the High Court, two judges from which sat to hear it. The hearing took many days. The judges were Gorman and McNair, JJ. For the petitioners, there appeared Sir Andrew Clark, Q.C., H. P. J. Milmo, Q.C. and D. G. Widdicombe. Benn appeared in his own cause. Also R. H. W. Dunn was present on behalf of the Director of Public Prosecutions. The summary of the judgement, which was a reserved one, was: 'Held: on the evidence before the court, the facts which in law created the respondent's incapacity to be elected a Member of Parliament were known to the electors before they cast their votes and the court was, therefore, bound to declare that the votes case for the respondent had been thrown away and that the petitioner was duly elected as the Member of Parliament for the constituency.' (*All England Law Reports, re Bristol South East Parliamentary Election.*)

The plain meaning of this is that Benn is Stansgate who is not the M.P. for Bristol, S.E., but Malcolm Sinclair is. The latter, therefore sits as Member for a constituency where a majority of the electors have voted against him. As the judgement is final, the only hope of Stansgate is in a change in the law which will permit him to relinquish his peerage and stand again for the seat.

This judgement will go down in peerage history as a memorable *cause célèbre*. In fact it is the most important since the Rhondda case in 1922 when the court under the Lord Chancellor, the 1st

Earl of Birkenhead, decided that peeresses in their own right could not sit in the House of Lords. In view of the fact that women had been allowed to sit up all night in the Commons as M.P.s, it seems more than a little strange that they should not be allowed the privilege of the gentlemanly chamber next door. However, the 1922 judgement was a remarkable milestone in peerage law, and this will be equally true of the 1961 Stansgate case. In each instance the student of the peerage and of peerage law will find in it a mine of useful information about the meaning of peerage. Yet what is the value of all this learning when the decision of this august court can be at variance with common sense and modern demands?

For that is the position. The people of Bristol voted for the man of their choice. He is ousted because the law is against him. His opponent, defeated in the ballot, still takes his place as the Member of those who voted against him.

Here is the clearest case in which the old time rules have determined a matter which is essentiallly modern. Beyond any doubt Viscount Stansgate knows that he is a peer – there have been peerage claimants who would have given five years of life to establish their peerage pretensions with the certainty which has been accorded him, unsought. But all that this means is that Stansgate is to be a peer willy nilly. No one can be forced to receive an inheritance which he does not want. Suppose a man living in Croydon is told of a legacy from a friend, of a house in Caithness. He is at first overjoyed that he can inherit the property and make some money by the sale. But no, the condition of the gift is that he is to live in the house. Of course he declines the benefaction. Nothing can compel him to accept it. Yet when it comes to a peerage, the situation is quite different. Wedgwood Benn does not want to live, politically, in the regions of the Upper House. He wishes to continue in the Commons. But he is not allowed to. He must belong to the Lords.

Here is a repudiation of the will of the people, and one can be little surprised that in the heat of a by-election, as well as in the soberness which follows a court decision, the case is widely regarded as one of the Lords versus the people of Bristol. For that is exactly what it was, or to put it another way, the law, antiquated and out-of-touch with modern affairs, versus the will of the electors.

It is true that a commission or committee is promised on the subject of Lords' Reform, but my opinion is that little will happen from this source – the names of the members are not yet given. When it is appointed – if ever – what will its terms of reference be? Wide enough to consider those peers who may wish to surrender their peerages? Or just the same old re-hash for keeping the House of Lords in being, in a slightly changed form?*

Another and less obtrusive form of the dilemma which confronts the titled system can be found in the attitude adopted towards foreign titles. How are they to be regarded in our system of nobility? Ths historic attitude towards them has always been the same, that our sovereigns have not cared much for their own subjects accepting foreign decorations and honours. The rule is clear that before such acceptance can take place, permission must be sought from the reigning sovereign. There is a classic case in which Queen Elizabeth I did not much like one of her nobles, Lord Arundel of Wardour, whose peerage died out in the last war, accepting a Countship of the Holy Roman Empire from the Emperor to whom he had rendered good service in war. Because Lord Arundel did not ask her consent to the honour (perhaps because he knew it would be refused) she imprisoned him.

What, however, of foreign titles borne by persons who have come to this country from a foreign land and who have become British subjects? Their case is different from that of the native-born subject, but the rule has always been as with the previous class of people for several centuries, that they should seek permission from the sovereign before using their titles. This has applied as much to coats of arms as to titles of nobility. Nor should the title be used until the permission has passed through the formal channels and gone to the College of Arms. Yet today there are numerous British subjects who in their countries of origin possessed a title of nobility, and who are often addressed by that title in informal reference, e.g., in the newspapers; despite all this, these persons do not figure in any reference work with the title to which they were entitled at birth. Two well-known examples can be given. One often hears of Prince Frederick of Prussia. He is the grandson of the Kaiser, and the son of the famous 'little Willie'. He is a British subject, living and farming in England, married to a British wife. In formal circles, he is not Prince Frederick but Mr Mansfield, or whatever surname he may have used in the past. Reference to him as Prince Frederick are matters of courtesy only.

* Since writing this book it appears that the surrender of life peerages *will* be considered.

Then there is the instance of Baron Nugent. His title comes from the old Austrian Empire. He was offered a contract in the U.S.A. and, of course, as often happens with British folk in the Americas, the title was helpful in securing the contract. But, unfortunately, he was quizzed by newspaper reporters before he set sail. He was referred to by them as Lord Nugent. Now this was quite incorrect. In England a baron, of the British peerage, is correctly termed Lord X. But a continental baron is never so described. He is always Baron Y. Consequently, when he found himself called Lord Nugent, Baron Nugent was obviously constrained to alter the description. As soon as it was known that he was not a Lord, the contract failed to materialise.

Agreed that there must be some regulation of the foreign titles used in this land by those who have put themselves under the protection of the British Throne. Then let the regulation be clear and understood by all concerned. But what is the actual position? In 1932 there did come out from King George V a very clear regulation on the matter. Why is it not acted upon? Because it is not known. Why is it unknown? Because it has been smothered, there is no other term for the virtual disappearance of the document in which the King declared his will and pleasure.

The story unfolded somewhat like this: At a conference of Commonwealth or Empire Premiers, King George V noticed that two of them were wearing decorations which he did not immediately recognise. These turned out to be Papal orders. I believe that the two in question were worn by the Premiers of Ireland and Australia. There has been ever since the Reformation a dislike of Papal honours in this country on the part of the Establishment, and an unwillingness to recognise them, at least in the case of British subjects. Therefore, King George V having considered the matter issued a Royal Warrant in 1932, the wording of which was extremely frank. It was intended, so ran the Warrant, that foreign titles should in due time cease to be used by British subjects. All the licences which existed, from previous sovereigns, were revoked, and yet in order to make the change more gradual and accommodating, a schedule to the Warrant was added, in which some thirty-nine instances were given in which the titles were to be allowed. Such allowance was, however, only for the life of the holder of the title, plus the life of his son and grandson. It was all very clear and there has been no change in the royal arrangements since 1932.

Now, when I came to edit *Burke's Peerage* after the war and was engaged in clearing up one section after another, I came upon the Foreign Titles section, in which all manner of names appeared, with a little note tucked safely away under the heading. According to this, foreign titles borne by British subjects strictly speaking required a licence from the Crown. When I examined this section I was quite sure that there were names included which had never received a licence. My researches led, with the assistance of the College of Arms, to the discovery of the Royal Warrant of 1932. In the case of such a Warrant, it was the custom to direct it to the Duke of Norfolk, as head of the College, so that it could be enrolled in the registers there. When I found it, it appeared to have been buried, so little was known about it. No one appeared to be satisfied. I received a number of complaints from those whose titles I had excluded. I received many queries from newspapers and other sources, who found it difficult to understand the matter. I considered it further and thought that the most simple way of dealing with the subject was to print the Royal Warrant. I had no idea of the obstacles which were to be placed in my way. First from the College of Arms, then from the Home Office, and from all other quarters. It seemed that the Warrant was something recondite or rather something to be ashamed of, and which must not be revealed. It belonged to a kind of *arcanum fidei;* only the initiates could be admitted within the veil. At length a high official went out of his way to explain the position to me. While the late King had wished, so this official explained, to rout out foreign titles, and while, of course, his Warrant was the final authority, it had been felt that it would be unkind to many persons to wipe out their titles publicly. Thus it came about that although foreign titles were frowned on at Court, in effect nothing was to be done about them, and the Royal Warrant became of no effect. It was, it appears, never promulgated.

The ensuing confusion is considerable. No one knows where he is in the matter of foreign titles. Those few persons who have copies of the relevant document, i.e., the Royal Warrant, are not able to make use of them. The result of all this is that the use of foreign titles in England follows no consistent rule. How can it, when the document which governs the whole subject is kept as though it were some grave secret of the State? The Royal Warrant on the use of foreign titles is indeed, in the American phrase used so much in the war, Top Secret.

This sort of thing is so typical of the ramshackle workings of our

Establishment that it illustrates perfectly the dilemmas which confront all those who honestly or hypocritically wish to preserve it. It stretches, it creaks, it is torn in parts, yet there are those who criticise any attempt to take it away and substitute for it a rational and coherent scheme. Don't do away with the traditions of England, they say, but how can it be argued that something which is no longer true should be kept going?

Some few years ago a decision in the English courts gave yet another proof of the strange inconsistencies to which we can be conducted by those who manage our Establishment. It has been pointed out that there is a little known or understood division of peerages, that of suspended peerages. Under the Titles Deprivation Act of 1917, certain persons who happened to be at the same time peers of Great Britain and also in arms against the British sovereign, were deprived of their privileges and titles, on the ground that they had been enemies of the realm in the First World War. But the Act did not end their peerages. These people were prevented from having their names on the roll of peers, and from using their titles in the British dominions. But the titles themselves were not taken away, in the sense in which they are taken away when a man is condemned for high treason. Thus the sons of one whose title had been reduced in this way could petition the sovereign on a subsequent occasion to have the titles restored. The three concerned were the 2nd Duke of Albany, the 3rd Duke of Cumberland, and the 13th Viscount Taaffe.

Now in 1955 and 1956 an interesting case came before the English courts. This was the application of Prince Ernest of Hanover, the heir of the Duke of Cumberland, to be declared a British subject. He had not borne arms against the British sovereign in the Second World War, and it was thought that he should rightly be declared a British subject as indeed he was by the British courts. But if on the reasoning adopted Prince Ernest was British, then so were many other continental royalties who shared as he did in the Blood Royal of this country. It was estimated that some 400 persons could easily be involved. It was even suggested that the famous Kaiser Wilhelm the Second, the German ruler of the First World War, had been a British subject!

Here once more is another instance of the manner in which, because of our refusal to consider a full-scale revision of our titled and honours system, we blunder on into nonsense. If the Titles Deprivation Act did not end these foreign-held peerages, then the matter should be cleared up, either by the present heir being allowed the title, or by a clarification of the situation which would remove the title and clear up the anomaly. It may be added that Prince Ernest of Hanover has not sought to have the peerage revived to which he is heir.

Before passing on to consideration of possible reforms which would give us an Establishment suited to modern times, it may be asked how the honours of our system have stood as regards corruption and financial bribery. There is a history, extending over three centuries, of the sale of honours. It began with James I. This sovereign had many disadvantages in inheriting the English throne. He had none of the skill of his cousin, the great Elizabeth I. He had trouble with his parliaments almost from the beginning of his reign in England. Moreover, appearances were deceptive for him. He had been used to terrible intrigues and brutal conspiracies against his person in Scotland, and when he came to England he found the people at first apparently very submissive. This, naturally, gave him the idea that he was of greater importance than he really was. He adopted all sorts of high-flown ideas about his prerogative, but towards the end of his reign he realised that he was not going to have such an easy passage, especially when he wanted money. He bequeathed a hard situation and a bad example to his son, Charles I. James had begun to sell honours. During the period from 1603, the date of James's accession, to 1629, no less than seventy-two peers were made. This was double the number that James had found on his accession. He died in 1625 but his son, Charles I, though personally honourable, and unwilling to sell the peerage, was forced by economic necessity to do so.

Under James I, the order of baronets was instituted, as already mentioned, and this operation was from beginning to end a financial move. Then the actual sale of honours set in. Charles I endeavoured to stop it, but he was forced to create a new order or branch of the baronets' order in the case of Nova Scotia, where he needed money, and then found that here were persons willing to pay a lump sum for the exercise of the royal prerogative of making peers, baronets and knights.

Some very interesting accounts of financial transactions of this nature down the years are given in Gerald MacMillan's book, *Honours for Sale*. This work, published in 1954, has for its sub-title, The Strange Story of Maundy Gregory. The latter, at one time the proprietor of *Burke's Landed Gentry*, had gone full scale into the procurement of honours for those who were willing to pay. He acted as a sort of agent or broker, and was said to have made £30,000 per year when at the height of his power.

From Stuart kings to Maundy Gregory is a long step. The explanation of the change is due to the fact that whereas under the Stuarts the sale of honours lay between king and subject, by the time of Maundy Gregory the exercise of the royal prerogatives had largely passed into the hands of the government of the day, and of the Prime Minister. Consequently, the latter-day traffic in honours was far worse. In the 1600s, a purchase of a title was merely a straightforward way of getting what one wanted from the only person able to gratify one's feelings. With the passing of the Stuarts, the power of sale, as in so many matters, passed to the Ministers of the Crown, rather than the Crown itself. Now, it is much more difficult for a minister to open up shop for peerages titles, than for a monarch. The competence to create formally the peer or baronet is not in the power of the minister. Although the minister is the ruler of the realm, in fact, he still is not the creator of honours, a matter which in a monarchical country, is the prerogative of the sovereign.

When, therefore, venality in the granting of peerages does in modern times emerge, it is marked with graft of a very unpleasant nature. All those responsible band together to disclaim any responsibility for the sale of honours. The theory is that the honours come out in the twice-yearly lists because of merit, but the facts show that when the patronage of honours passed from monarch to ministers, some very businesslike transactions occurred.

The full story of the sale of honours is too long to be detailed or even outlined here. It will be found in the book quoted above, to which the reader should refer.

Suffice to say that a Political Honours Scrutiny now exists; this is a committee of three Privy Counsellors; also we have the Honours (Prevention of Abuses) Act, 1925. Only one prosecution has taken place under the Act, that of Maundy Gregory, but it has been sufficient. The sale of peerages appears to have ended with the fall of Lloyd George in 1922, that of baronetcies and knighthoods went on for some years longer, but this too came to an end in 1933, when Gregory was sent to prison.

Thus in one very important respect we can say that there has been progress, in stopping the sale of honours. So long had this practice lasted, however, that it might almost have been claimed as a tradition of Britain; for many of our most cherished traditions have a life of far less than the 330 years since the British Solomon began to hawk titles around in return for cash.

Since this chapter was written, there has occurred another case of inheritance by an M.P. of a peerage. Lord Hinchingbrooke, M.P. for South Dorset, has fallen heir to his father's title of the Earldom of Sandwich. He does not want to go into the Lords. Can nothing be done to make some arrangement to suit these cases? The Committee which is to consider and report on such cases is now in being, with its terms of reference limited, so it is understood, to the question of the surrender, whether temporary or permanent, of peerages. But it is clear that peerage surrender if it comes in will not be limited to members of one political party.

CHAPTER FIFTEEN

Reforms

IN this book I have tried to give a picture of what is meant by the Establishment. I am conscious that much has been left out. In fact, the more I think about the matter, and I have taken the time to think, the more convinced I am that it is virtually impossible to deal with every aspect of our Establishment in one book. It touches the lives of almost everyone in this country, in some capacity or another.

I do not think that there can be any doubt that some of the aspects of the Establishment need to be changed. I do not advocate mere change as such. I am sure that a conservative (with a small c) attitude is right, provided that it is not allowed to dominate all one's thoughts. Unless a country is hopelessly misgoverned, there is some value in conserving whatever is good from the past. To conserve the good while removing the bad or useless – that surely is the aim of all sincere and true reformers. To make real progress while retaining whatever is valuable from the former days, that is no doubt very difficult, but it is the true aim which we should strive to attain. It has always been the rule in this country, with the exception of the period under Puritan domination. By means of this attitude we have successfully weathered storms which have overwhelmed other nations. We have given full democratic franchise to all at twenty-one without chopping off any heads, and without confiscation of property. We still have much inequality in our country, nor am I suggesting that it is wrong. We still have titles in England, while legislative power rests with the untitled, and that is all to the good. But there is now the need for many reforms.

I think that the two great ills which can be perceived from a consideration of the Establishment are that first of all it is a perpetuation in many instances of things which no longer have any validity. In many cases we have failed to distinguish between the pageantry of tradition, and the clogging hand of former days.

Then the second trouble with which we are afflicted is that of worship of the past. We very often forget our history and its immense

value as a source of national strength. Yet we are held up at every turn
with some vestige of a past which was often far from lovely, or even
useful. Sometimes a road needs to be widened, but there are some
ancient cottages standing beside it. These must not be touched, and
so only a partial widening takes place.

While I was thinking over this book, I happened to walk up the
steps from the Horse Guards to Downing Street. Although it was
evening the hum of work had not ceased, and the famous garden
and building of No. 10 resembled nothing so much as some small
industrial plant which was in full blast. When I got in front of the
famous entrance, I read a notice which said that the building was
being reconstructed, but that the famous Cabinet Room, etc.,
plus the façade of the house would be preserved. There is a lesson
here. I agree that it is worth a lot of effort to keep the historic appearance of the building from outside. Inwardly it is being reconstructed,
except for the Cabinet Room, and will be a modern building. This
extensive remodelling has been necessitated by the demands of
modern life. The residence of the Prime Ministers of this country is
of historic interest, but life was less exacting in the eighteenth century,
and even in the nineteenth. The old house is now not good enough
for the heavy tasks imposed upon it. It would have been easy to
have swept it aside, and to have replaced it with something stream-
lined and box-like, in keeping with so many of the buildings whose
towers are now disfiguring the London skyline. It could also have
been patched up, or just left. The sensible alternative was however
adopted, to preserve its important appearance, and any essential
features, while remodelling the rest.

There is an example here for our politicians and social reformers.
If we look down the whole of our titled system, from Crown to plain
mister, we shall see today in most cases the essential and the inessential mingled together in such a way that old precedence takes
the place of modern need. There is a strange worship of the past
which makes me afraid that in some thirty or forty years' time, unless
there is an awakening, American visitors may be inclined to tour that
quaint little old country, England. 'Don't you know, Elmer, they
have the loveliest habits and customs? Last time we were in England,
junior wanted to see some of the real old-fashioned soldiers, and
that very nice colonel put on a show of his men just for us, so that
we could get some pictures.' Fantasy? Not so fantastic if we are not
careful. We could very easily begin to pride ourselves that we have a

great past, and that all we need to do is live in it. There have been such nations, and there is no compelling reason to prevent the same fate overtaking us.

In some of our traditional ways we have followed the example of No. 10 Downing Street. The Trooping the Colour, and the Queen's Opening of Parliament are two particular instances. We have already considered these, and shown that while the Trooping the Colour was in the seventeenth century of practical utility and used as such in the heat of battle, it has ceased to be considered of immediate practical value now. On the other hand its value as a means of building up national and military spirit remains very great. Similarly the progress of politics has made the State Opening of Parliament and the Gracious Speech from the Throne merely a pageant of the past position between Crown, Lords and Commons. Yet its value, especially now that it has been televised, is enormous. It shows as in a play the change which has come over our political system in the past four centuries. I have already gone into this in detail, but I am sure that these ceremonies have great value. Therefore I reiterate my mention of them.

We as a nation have in the past been peculiarly skilful in keeping the essential while discarding the non-essential or the positively harmful. We seem, however, to have lost this ability. Take, to start with, the problem of the monarchy. The deprivation of power which the monarchy has endured over the last 200 years has made it a figurehead, without real initiative. Even the last prerogative of the sovereign – to send for the political leader who is to form a government – is much less a real power than is often supposed in the frequent references to it.

But is this any justification for the present tendency to deify the Royal Family? It is a maxim of the constitution, far outside this country, as well as in it, that the Sovereign can do no wrong. This is a necessary precaution so that the ministers can take the blame for anything which happens to go wrong in the country. They must have tendered bad advice to the Crown. But this maxim was never meant to lead to the ossification of the monarchy, and to the growth of a Mikado-like royalty. Yet, it is just this process that is taking place at present in several instances. One of the outstanding examples is the bestowal of a title upon the husband of Princess Margaret. For this can only mean one thing; that today anyone who marries into the Royal Family spelt with capitals becomes *ipso facto* absolutely distinguished from the rest of us. By an odd coincidence, just previously another earldom had been created, that of Avon. Now, whatever views may be taken of Sir Anthony (the other Anthony) Eden's politics it is true that he rendered great and selfless services to his country. The guerdon of a retired Premier is an earldom. There can be few who grudged this elevation to one who has given of his best, including his health, to England. But the fact that an earldom was also bestowed upon Mr Armstrong-Jones before the birth of Princess Margaret's child is a prime example of the system which, it appears, requires him for this reason only to be ennobled.

Many small indications of the formality of the royal outlook can be found. As there is no royal power, so there is no royal spontaneity. The attitude of walking with hands folded behind, in the case of the royal men, is symptomatic of the Byzantinism of our royal house. It is now thirty years since one of our sovereigns exercised a perceptible influence on the course of events. That was in 1931 when, through the guidance of George V, the leaders of the political world were brought together to form the National Government. Nothing like this is likely to happen again. Since nothing is likely to reverse a process which has once set in, in the development of nations and their in-stitutions, we have to accept the fact that real power has left our monarchy. We cannot expect that one night the Sovereign should retire to rest, a modest and demure member of the House of Windsor, and wake next morning as a reincarnation of Bluff King Hal or Elizabeth the Great. But because the function of the Crown is now no longer direct, it does not mean that the British monarchy should become an imitation of the Japanese, where a semi-divine aura has surrounded the monarch, who has at the same time never been allowed any power and has sometimes in the long history of the Mikados been forced to live in humility and poverty.

The development of an excessive reverence for the monarchy is not a sign of strength but of dissolution. In many states just before their decline into republicanism there has been an unhealthy outbreak into a formal reverence for the sovereign and his or her surroundings which has been the sign of the approaching end. I feel that we can have a much freer and more democratic monarchy without going to the extent of the Swedish or other Scandinavian countries. They have made monarchy somewhat commonplace, and no one is surprised to find the King of Sweden standing beside him at a museum or ex-hibition. I do not think we shall ever come to this, but there is the danger of our being wrapped around with some strange mystery when we touch the monarchy. It is difficult to get this into exact words, but perhaps the concrete example of the royal yacht *Britannia* will serve. This vessel, it is always asserted, costs £1,000 per day to run. Well, when it is used for the transport of the Sovereign, it can be justified, if at all, on the plea that the head of the State should always travel in fitting style. But it is more difficult to justify when the vessel is used for a honeymoon in the Caribbean for Princess Margaret and her husband. It all comes down to the fact that a kind of royal caste is being built up which cannot possibly be made good in the revolutionary era in which we live. And if this goes on we might easily find ourselves equipped with a monarchy somewhat resembling those which formerly existed in the princely states of India where the ruling prince belonged to the Hindu religion and ruled over a majority of Moslems, or where vice versa a Moslem ruled over Hindus. The Royal Family here could become a sort of family apart entirely from the people they nominally govern or preside over.

Leaving the Royal Family for the present, we come to the main strength of the whole titled system, after the Crown, and that is the House of Lords. Here, as I have shown in my earlier chapters there exists the most extraordinary series of compromises, and patch-up policies. There is nothing logical or coherent in connection with the Lords. Little wonder that no one outside the country can grasp its meaning, and few of those inside England.

If we are ever going to have a sensible arrangement with regard to the Lords, it is no use tinkering with it any more. We should have a proper reform. By this I do not, of course, mean the abolition of the Lords. The reform of the Lords is not a matter of abstruse meditation. It requires only a clear coherent policy. For the future do not create more hereditary peers. Not that there is any objection as such to hereditary titles, except when they are not able to be renounced! But there is no longer any possibility of large estates or considerable wealth being handed on. To create more hereditary lords is only to make up a kind of nobility of the gutter, or perhaps it would be more appropriate to say of the semi-detached flat, and the poorly-paid clerical job.

The existing hereditary peerages could be left untouched, of course, for what justice is there in prohibiting a man from inheriting an honour if he wishes to have it? Equally, as with the Wedgwood Benn case, there should be provision for the surrender of the peerage by those who wish to do so. I have pointed out that this right of surrender did exist in times past, that it is no longer the law, and that it should be revived. As to the difficulty of reviving it, that need occasion no trouble. When a law is wanted, it is at once forthcoming.

Then having decided not to create any more hereditary peerages, we should make up our minds clearly what sort of House of Lords we really want. Should it continue any longer to be known as the Lords, or should it be known as the Upper House, or Senate? These are matters for considerable debate. But they can be settled by reasonable discussion. The composition of the House of Lords would, in the event that no more hereditary peerages were created, become more democratic. Life peerages could be the rule. As to the existing hereditary peerages, a proportion of them could be retained in the reformed House, who would be chosen, as the Scottish peers are now, by voting among the peers themselves. This is the extent to which I was at one time prepared to go in the reform of the Lords; no more hereditary peerages, only life peers to be created, and along with them in a revised House, a number of hereditary peers, chosen from among their fellows by vote. But would this really meet the situation? Life peerages are not terribly democratic. A life peer might be very bright at forty and a washout at sixty. If he were elected only for a term of years, he could be got rid of in the same way as a Member of the Commons. I recall that when the first batch of life peers came along, one of my friends remarked that I should not be overtroubled in one or two cases because the recipient of the honour was not likely to live long.

Here then is another argument to consider on the subject of life peerages. A life peer is not likely to assist us much if he is too old, when appointed, to be able to discharge the obligations successfully. If, on the other hand, he is too young and thus has some thirty or forty years of life, during which he becomes increasingly a bore, the purpose of his appointment, unless it is limited in time, will then become likewise frustrated.

It seems, therefore, to me that the best course is to appoint the British senators for a term of years, in short, in the same way as the American and Australian senators are (in Canada senators are appointed for life). In that case, of course, we should not want the term 'Lords'. There would be no need of Lords as such. They could simply be senators, who sat for five or ten years. This would give much better results. They could be elected on a ratepayers basis.

Then what would happen to the hereditary peers? There would be nothing to prevent them from offering themselves for election by the said ratepayers. I am also a great believer in pageantry. There could be a mock House of Lords with debates and ceremonies which would have no effect on the Government, but would successfully maintain the traditional past.

We should replace the existing House of Lords with an Upper House, which, of course, it is in name. But this Upper House, being on the lines of the Senates in the three great democracies of U.S.A., Canada, and Australia, would have some power. It is quite absurd to suppose that an Upper House, a Second Chamber, is merely meant to be a revising rubber stamp institution. It should have, and usually does in democratic states have, some function of reviewing legislation, and initiating it, also of, quite frankly, holding it up when it is considered that second thoughts are best. True, the present House of Lords can hold up legislation, and has done so in recent years, but its power to do so is limited to one year, and a bill which it rejects automatically becomes law if put forward one year later. Therefore, it is an accepted technique among Left-Wing politicians that a very controversial measure shall be put up to the Lords early within their terms of office, thus ensuring its passage into law, despite rejection for twelve months by the Lords.

Would the abolition of the House of Lords as at present constituted mean the end of peerages? By no means. Hereditary peerages for reasons given, are in my view, inadmissible for the future. The fact that we are creating them still, is no argument for their continuance. Further hereditary peerages would mean only that there would be a growing number of cases similar to that of Wedgwood Benn. His instance has received great publicity because he has tried to remain in the House of Commons, but there are dozens of peers already who do not achieve a like renown but who quietly abandon their titles and melt away into the realm of Misterdom. During my editorship of *Burke* I often received requests from peers to leave them out of my records because they did not use their titles. In one case, that of the late Lord Langford, he bound me never to write to him other than as Mr Rowley. He was employed as a night watchman and lived in a tenement. His neighbours, he said, were decent folk and it would injure him with them if they knew he was a lord.

Life peerages should be the only ones created for the future. They can be given for successful achievement in the different walks of life.

They can form the staple of the honours lists of the future. The mere lack of a seat in the Lords is not going to dim the lustre of a title. It is in the social sphere and not in the political that a title has relevance and value. Besides, there will be no barrier for the lord as such to election in the Senate. He will have every means of canvassing for a seat in the Senate, and for being elected thereto by the ratepayers. In fact many of those, like the present Marquess of Salisbury, who are men of ability in their own right, will win their way into the new Upper House.

There are many countries where titles are no longer conferred by their governments but where the use of titles persists. Because of the failure of the respective governments to notice titles, the nobles of these lands (Italy is a case in point) band themselves together to register the titles so that impostors should not be able to take advantage of them.

No loss of anything essential would result from the proposals which I have put forward. We should all gain, because a strong and efficient Upper House – and no one can at the moment claim either of these attributes for the Lords – would assist very greatly in the government of the country, and would allow of titles as such being given their proper value as marks of guerdon for services done.

At the same time it is important for the traditional past to be kept up. As I have pointed out in the ceremonial usages such as the State Opening of Parliament, and the Trooping the Colour, we have the advantage of maintaining the traditional while at the same time not allowing it to take the place of something more utilitarian. The same process must be extended to our semi-feudal institutions such as the Lords. There can be, as suggested, a House of Lords which can reproduce the settings of the nineteenth and earlier centuries. This will show people who are interested what it all looked like in bygone days. I have known grown-up men take the Hampstead Parliament very seriously. The debates at Oxford and Cambridge in the respective Unions are serious matters; no one who breaks a rule is likely to get away with it. There are ceremonial clothes to be worn by those who preside. Yet we do not allow the Unions to take part in government. Nor should we allow the Lords, but the debates which they could stage would be just as valuable or more so than at present. Just as the debates of the 'Varsity Unions are an index to the feeling of the new generation, so the debates in the old House of Lords would be a warning signal of the views advocated by a conservative section of the population. Meanwhile, the Senate would get on with the job of helping to run the Government.

As to the great officers of State, here again we should need the hand of reform. It is so silly to keep a table of precedence which is headed (after the Royal Family) with imaginary posts, posts that is which existed once but no longer have any reference to modern times. I am all in favour of the old historic titles (Admiral of the Coasts of the Bristol Channel, or of the Shores of Westmorland and Cumberland) being retained. No one expects that any duty should attach to such things, but in a properly organised state we could have super pageants; e.g., in Bristol it would be fascinating to see the hereditary Admiral of the Shores of the Bristol Channel leading a fleet of frail vessels (the men-of-war of the fourteenth century) against a French invasion. What an object lesson for the pupils in State schools! They would learn their history more easily. But such titles have no active relevance to modern conditions.

In the case of the Earl Marshal, his office is still in function, and I have shown that it is of sufficient importance to warrant proper support from the State. With the Earl Marshal relieved of his worries over money, attention could be turned to his official establishment, the College of Arms. This needs to be placed on a proper establishment footing, so that it can deal adequately with the potentially enormous volume of business which can flow in from all over the English-speaking world. The records of the College should be administered by civil servants who will be as quick in their work as their existing counterparts in the offices of Somerset House, etc. While they administer the records, and conduct the routine inquiries, the Officers of Arms will be free to get on with the business of ceremonies, and of learned research into pedigrees and coats of arms. They will retain the power to deal with arms, but this power will be covered by Acts of Parliament as in Scotland, with, of course, a regular scale of fees. It follows as a necessary corollary that the Officers of Arms will receive salaries, instead of the feeble remuneration at present which necessarily has to be supplemented by charging dues for granting arms.

The Table of Precedence is an inevitable accompaniment in any state, and where it has not existed, as with some new countries, it has soon been found necessary to produce one. The present 400-years-outdated Table in England could be brought up to date without using more than a tithe of the learned ingenuity now required by experts to explain it and to find places within it for those who were never recognised in the time of Henry VIII, or even George I.

It is too late now to call a halt to the spoliation of the landed gentry, but something could be done to help estates which are larger than the single farm. They could be given some tax reliefs (the lower rates of death duty on land have not prevented the break-up of estates), and thus enabled to survive as a single unit. Where the relics of the old system survive, we see that enormous benefits have been conferred upon the country. Even the English landscape has been to some extent created by the care and skill of the large landed proprietor. A Park like that at Woburn would have been impossible under a regime of small peasant proprietors. We know, of course, that the big landed gentry class cannot any longer go on as the sole dispensers of culture and refinement in an area. The big house cannot be the centre of the district any more. Nonetheless there is still value to be gained from the presence within a district of a large house with lands surrounding it, which is kept as one economic unit. It should be by no means impossible to keep some part of the old landed gentry aristocracy by the simple device of letting the land be tax-free. In the Rating and Valuation Act 1928 and the Local Government Act 1929 agricultural land was derated and this gave a great encouragement to farming. In the same way we could very easily give relief to the relics of the landed gentry class before the night descends upon them. To give cash grants to maintain historic houses is not snobbish. I have explained what few people seem able to understand who are outside that social stratum, that the aristocracy of this country, unlike that of continental Europe, is composed of untitled as well as titled persons, in fact some of the untitled families are much older and nobler than those which possess peerages and baronetcies.

Coming to the great section of the Establishment which is properly the Establishment, the national Church of England, we reach the stage where the question of moral and spiritual values becomes of utmost importance. There is throughout the rank and file of Church members a feeling that all is not well within the Church, and this with particular reference to the methods of appointment of bishops and deans. It is too painfully obvious that the Church is staffed at the top by many who have no pastoral experience and who are out of touch with the feelings and wishes of the majority of those to whom they minister as chief pastors.

It seems to me that the only way for the Church of England to regain its hold over the nation is by deciding once and for all what it wishes to teach. It has, of course, in *The Thirty-Nine Articles*, the statement of its belief, and it should either proceed to enforce these or else draw up a new code of belief. This new code should be very clearly an expression of old beliefs in new form. In one sense there is no progress in Christianity. It contains a faith once for all delivered to the Saints, and this cannot be altered for the convenience of modern views, which today are and to morrow are outmoded.

Perhaps, as I have been inclined to say in the special chapter given to this subject, the best way out of the present difficulties, is to dis-establish the Church and to make it free of the State, so that it can regulate its own affairs as it please, in conformity with the law of Christ. But if Establishment is to continue then it must be with greater freedom than there is now.

The affairs of the Church of England are enormously complicated. Establishment is no new thing in the history of the English Church and English nation. From the very first days of Christianity in this country the Church has been allied closely with the nation, from the days when the Church had a unity which the State, rent and divided into seven kingdoms, did not possess. At the great crises of the nation's life, the Church was ever in the forefront. When the Refor-mation came to divide Englishmen in their religious views, hardly anyone thought that a new Church was being set up. Gradually the idea has gained ground that there was some kind of mysterious change, when overnight, at some unspecified date, the Church of England became Protestant from being formerly Roman Catholic. Yet it would be hard for anyone to point out when this great event occurred. As late as 1660–62 there was still the intent to keep all the nation inside the Church. The Puritans, while they decided that they had no time for the rule of bishops, yet wished to have all Christians within one fold. Oliver Cromwell was considered most remarkable in that he gave toleration to all who were not openly Papists or Prelatists. Even Papists were tolerated under this rule, if they kept their worship within doors. His Cavalier opponents not only gained a poor triumph over his dead body when they hung it on a tree at Tyburn, but overthrew his principles of toleration. The various Acts of Parliament which were passed at the accession of Charles II, such as the Test Act and the Conventicles Act, were per-secution, with the object of compelling all Christians to remain within the one Church. They failed, and from 1662 we have to date the sad divisions of Englishmen into Church of England, Non-Conformists, and the rest. This division of the religious world persisted into the present century, but now we are all much more polite to each other, and refer to Church of England, to Anglicans (I am sure there are some educated persons who do not know that the descriptions are identical), Free Churches, and Roman Catholics.

Today the myriad sects and Churches are a source of immense trouble within England. It is very hard to convey the idea of a solid body of Christian truth, when there are over 300 different forms of it within the boundaries of little England. Within the Church of England itself, the three-hundred-year-old separation from some one-third of the people of the country, who own other religious allegiance than to the State Church, has produced a latitude of opinion which is quite bewildering. High Church and Low Church, Broad Church and Modernist, they are more like parties within a political grouping than members of the same Church. But I am convinced that this diversity has come about through the inability of the national Church to control its own affairs. In no other Christian body is there such diversity of belief. True, all Christian bodies are plagued with modernism – the belief that the Christian Creed, the faith once delivered to the Saints can be tampered with and brought up to date at the behest of Science, which today is and tomorrow is forgotten – but no other Church is so torn by internecine feuds as the Anglican. This is simply and solely because it is not allowed to manage its own affairs. The example of the 1927 Prayer Book to which I have referred earlier is sufficient to prove this. The liturgical chaos within the Established Church is a grave disservice to the unhappy persons who drop into a church just by chance, moved by the spiritual impulse of the moment. They simply do not know what type of service they will meet. Even the ecclesiastical habitué will often be at a loss for a few minutes to know what the structure of the service will be, and whether, e.g., at Morning Prayer the first lesson will be omitted. As for the variations in the Holy Communion these are sometimes as numerous as the parishes within a single town.

The difficulties in the appointment of bishops and the other higher ranking ecclesiastics of which much is heard from time to time, and particularly at present, is only the highest wave in a sea of dissension and spiritual failure which is caused by the icy hand of the State upon the Church. *Ecclesia Anglicana* has failed to be a Teaching Church – *Ecclesia Docens* – and been too willing to be a huge debating society, with the result that she has lost the allegiance of multitudes of her children. But any attempt to regain her teaching standards is always hampered by the fact that the State will not permit the Church to order her own affairs, and also because many of the prelates appointed by the State agency are not themselves completely orthodox, that is judged by any standard of orthodoxy known in the historic Church of East and West, which, let it be remembered by those who deride the possibility of Christian unity, was one and united for 1,000 years.

It would seem, then, that among the necessary reforms with which we are concerned in this chapter, that of the Disestablishment and cleaning-up of the Church is one of the most important. In fact it is the most important. For we can stagger on for perhaps some considerable time, in a world of ever declining British influence with all the ridiculous paraphernalia of lords, and precedence and outdated ideas of social distinction. In that case we would simply be sinking ever lower into an abyss from which we could not emerge. But even this would not be as bad as our constantly growing lack of spiritual things, which results from the failure of the Church to touch the national life at every point.

With regard to the remaining sections of the life of the Establishment with which I have tried to deal in this book – the legal system, the House of Commons, the City of London, and various other spheres with which the English V.I.P. is conversant – reform here can only wait on a recrudescence of the national spirit, of which at present there is no sign. With the advent of democracy fewer and fewer persons are taking any interest in politics. On the other hand, there is an immense multiplication of laws which has rendered the very conception of law – once regarded as well-nigh sacred – meaningless. The law now interferes with so many matters where its entry cannot be viewed as either sensible or salutary that to the ordinary man or woman the old idea of law as being based on the Divine Law (I remember hearing it still so described by an M.P. in a public speech in 1929) has become unintelligible. It all looks so like an affair of orders by the minister who hears appeals in his own cause that the sanctity of law is gone.

It is when we turn to the City of London, great and magnificent as it is, that we may perhaps feel most mournful. Of late years the authorities in the City have shown themselves very anxious to promote the good image of the City. Much excellent work is being done by the City of London Society. This work is very necessary, if the

proper place of the City in the life of Britain is to be understood and
Left-Wing propaganda countered as it should be. Lecturers go out
under the auspices of the Society and give lectures on various subjects, not necessarily about the City, but always acting as agents for
the Society in the sense that meetings and gatherings throughout
England are made aware of the City of London as an integral part
in the life of our country. Moreover, many excellent talks are given
every year on the functions of the City, and many people are members
of the Society who do not belong to the higher echelons of Class.

Yet the best propaganda is always that of deeds. The City of
London is unique in something which is not a claim to honour – the
fact that at night it is a city without inhabitants. This has only come
about within the last hundred years, and less than that. It is a change
which would have mightily discomfited our ancestors. Often when
I walk up Bread Street, I have thought of the great poet who was
born there. It would have seemed strange to John Milton that the
street of his birth, even before its desecration by German bombs,
would lose its human inmates after the hour of six. We have in the
City preferred business to family and humanity. The merchants'
ledger has displaced the family Bible. Great as is the pageantry and
admirable the City feasts, yet there is something missing. When the
guests come out of a great city hall, they turn into a wilderness.
This may be very pleasant for their chauffeurs but it is not a city in
any sense which ancient or modern city-dwellers would recognise.

The City of London may be taken as a not unfair representation
of what may happen to our whole land if we do not heed the urgent
warning to modernise the essentially alterable part of our make-up.
The City has great power, it is, as we are at present constituted,
essential to the economic well-being of every person in this country.
Yet the image which it presents to much of the world is that of
pageantry. Just as the city companies have often ceased to be living
functioning bodies, in which persons can only enter if they belong
to a special trade or occupation, so much of the City is now ancient
history, concerned with pageantry, which recalls the past.

We could as a nation become a species of Ruritania, which would
decline slowly into impotence and would hide its poverty behind
massive gold plate and flunkeys' liveries (borrowed, of course, for the
occasion). I can imagine, in my sadder moments, a nasal voice
describing a little old country which it had visited on its way back
from a European tour. 'Say, you should go to the little burg, it's

called England. Yeah, they even have a crown and jewels and all sorts of things called lords, wearing robes out of the movies. It's worth a two-day visit, but say, boy is there some poverty over there! Last time I went, the kids in the street were hanging round my knees for cents.'

Yes, it is a horrible vision. But if we do not pull ourselves out of our lethargy, and our absorption with material goods, turn to the spiritual side of life and really jerk ourselves into something more healthy, it is a picture which will come true.

CHAPTER SIXTEEN

The Way Upward

THERE will always be plenty of people who will object to any proposal for reform that it will not take place. Things have been going like this for so long, they will say, that nothing will happen, no matter how strenuously you argue or contend for it. This is only partially true. It does not follow that because change is piecemeal or slow that it does not take place. There have been an enormous number of changes already in our titled system, as I have shown in the various sections of my book, but as I have also shown they have been without direction, as though they had been forced upon a reluctant Establishment, as, of course, they have. Changes of a far-reaching character have been made, but without any proper philosophy to support them, so that they are never sufficiently radical.

The reason for this must be sought in something other than a defect of national character. The underlying reason for our apparent shiftlessness in this country is that we have lost our morale. Right up to the 1914 war we were actuated by principles which put things other than material before the ordinary affairs of life. In 1914 Englishmen in their millions came forward to defend their country and to uphold moral principles for which they were quite prepared to die. Unfortunately, too many of these high-minded men did die, and left no heirs. Theirs was the shattered generation, only a wounded portion of which came back to take their normal places in our life. Earl Baldwin referred to the missing generation. The Earl of Avon was one of three brothers, but he was the only one to return to civilian life. The others died on war service which he himself also endured.

However, although we as a country were spiritually impoverished by our heavy losses in the First World War, we would even without those losses have sooner or later run into trouble. The generation of the 1914 war was living on spiritual capital, and the supply of this, as of material capital, does not last for ever. The crisis from which we are suffering finds its root far back in the nineteenth century. A hundred years ago this country was profoundly religious and sure of itself as a Christian country. In 1851 the British were stirred into violent controversy by the suggestion that the Roman Catholic hierarchy should be restored in England. Restored it was but to the accompaniment of riots and violence towards individual Catholics. The England of that time was Protestant in a marked degree. Still, however much we may deplore this excess of zeal, it was a zeal for things of the spirit, and it had a Christian ethos. The Church of England was rent by fierce internal controversy, but both sides, both the Low and the High Church, would have been agreed on the main doctrines of Christianity. Eventually some of the High Church leaders, Newman and Manning and many others, withdrew to Rome. The fierce Protestant feeling engendered at this time would probably have brought about a stirring and revival in conventional Protestantism, but for a very serious event. This was the publication in 1859 of the *Origin of Species* by Charles Darwin. This was easily the most influential book of the period, and caused immense controversy. It was some years before the publication of the same writer's *Descent of Man*, in which kinship for man with the anthropoids was claimed, but the implications of Darwin's doctrine of evolution by natural selection was clear from the start. Darwin did not originate the idea of evolution. It had been thought of by several of the ancients, including St Augustine; Darwin's grandfather had also conceived the theory, but it was left to Darwin to bring it out with a wealth of apparent proof, and with a theory which explained evolution. It is worth noting that fourteen years before Darwin, the famous John Henry Newman, later a Cardinal of the Roman Church, had propounded as his *Development of Christian Doctrine*, a theory of evolution in applied to Christian dogma which was no less revolutionary than Darwin's theory, but in another sphere. In a matter of decades the idea of evolution had caught on and been applied to every department of thought, so that by now it has become part and parcel of our way of thinking.

One of the results of the Darwinian theory was to challenge the Biblical account of the creation of man. If man had developed from the same stock as the apes then he had risen in the scale; no Fall was necessary and none could be found in the ledges of geological strata uncovered by the scientists. With the Fall and Original Sin went also the idea of Redemption. Along with the destructive criticism of the early chapters of Genesis went a similarly violent attack on the New Testament. The origins of Christianity were soon subjected to a criticism on the part of writers like Ernest Renan in France and the Tübingen School in Germany.

Thus as a result of the conflict between science and religion, the Bible was dethroned from its former position of supreme eminence in our national life. Attempts to keep up its reading for the sake of the literary content of the Authorised Version did not succeed in maintaining reverence for the Bible, once its unique and sacred character had gone.

Within twenty years of the Darwinian controversy bursting upon the world, the authority of the Bible had been seriously undermined, and it has never in this country regained its former position. In other lands in Europe, such as France and Italy, the shock of the new theories was not so great because there the Catholics were not concerned primarily with an infallible Bible, but with an infallible Church. Of course if the Biblical authority was removed, then the Church had nothing to stand on. Yet impact was not felt so much for the reason that people had not relied as much on the Bible in Catholic lands as they had in England and other Protestant countries.

It is this which lies at the base of our uneasiness and lack of spiritual strength because the original source of our belief has been taken away. It is true that the scholars and writers of the Church of England have laboured with great diligence to show that new knowledge, both of science and of Biblical criticism has not really destroyed Christianity, but they have had a heavy task, for it is always easier to attack than to defend, and the impression created by easy phrases is much more lasting than that of worthwhile study. Few people are equipped to weigh the meaning of words, and the sweeping statements of the scientists carried all before them.

In fact, of course, there is very often little real science in the pronouncements of scientists, taking science in its original meaning, *Scientia*, knowledge. If it is conceded for the sake of argument that the first three chapters of Genesis are myth, it should also be conceded that the substituted history of early man is mostly myth too. There has been the outstanding case of the Piltdown Man. But this is not alone, for the Pekin Man has a good deal of the spurious about him, and this vague phantom is not strengthened when we are told, as we used to be told, that the Pekin is nearly as solid a reality as his Piltdown brother. The Australopithecinae of South Africa have been given up. Still they come, these alleged ancestors of man, sometimes with an ancestry of 10,000,000 years! Yet who would dare, outside the ranks of evolutionists to sketch out such a faulty pedigree for early man? It is the rubbish which appears in most books on early man, which we are asked to take as a substitute for the account in the Bible.

A huge canvas has been laid out and painted over with almost entirely imaginary scenes of what life was like; the only base for this has been the discovery of bones here and bones there, as though it did not matter where the remains came from, and how mixed up they were; the effort on the imagination has been staggering, but it is ridiculous to call it scientific. Nor do the scientists, as far as one can see, give the impression of being actuated solely by zeal for truth. It is unwise for any scientist to query the theory of natural selection or of evolution. He might lose standing with his brethren. If this is not on a par with the vain pride of the medieval scholastics, I should be surprised. There are fashions in learning as in everything else. In the fourteenth century one followed Aristotle and did not go outside his pages, today it is perilous for one's reputation to query Darwin's views.*

The apparent triumph of the evolutionary hypothesis and the highly coloured picture derived from it has given an impression of a Bible record discredited. This conception has been aided by the growth of a Biblical criticism which was for a long time very destructive. The books of the Bible have been said to be a mixture of several hands, all very incompetent, be it added, in their editing. The first books of the Bible, hitherto for many ages described as the books of Moses, have been dissolved, on this view, into a mixture of authors denoted by P and J and D, etc. Similarly, the Gospels have been broken up into sources which may appear clear to the initiate but which to the ordinary writer look like ravings from the Bacon-is-Shakespeare controversy. German and other critics write and talk as though they really knew what happened in the gaps between the books of the New Testament, and as though they indeed knew more about the subject matter of the books than the authors themselves.

The modern world picture is one of a universe of enormous age

---

* On the Subject of Evolution, see a book by a Roman Catholic priest, *Science of Today and the Problems of Genesis*, by the Rev. Patrick O'Connell, 1959 (Radio Replies Press Society, St Paul, Minnesota). Also the introduction to the new Everyman edition of Darwin's *Origin of Species*, with an introduction by Mr Thompson, F.R.S., who does not agree with Darwin's ideas.

(contrasted, that is, with the length of human life and the 6,000 years which were regarded as the span of this planet until about a century ago). Not only is the universe extended in time; it is of formidable dimensions in space. It is inconceivably vast. Though there are speculations which represent the universe as finally limited in extent, there is a strong school which thinks of it in terms of continuous creation. The world goes on and on. It had, these thinkers contend, no beginning and will have no end; only the finite islands in this infinite universe change and disappear. Thus our earth and our solar system could disappear and probably will without the end of human life causing any disturbance in the universe as a whole. Sometimes we are told of a nova, i.e., a burnt-out star the light from which reaches us after an incredibly long journey, and which is supposed to represent a lost world.

Needless to say, the scientific possibilities of the vast universe in which we now find ourselves have been seized by the fiction writers who have explored practically every avenue of the imagination. Their imagination is, of course, bounded by their human condition, so that the forms of other life which may exist on other worlds, are subject to what can be thought up from our own environment. If and when space travel becomes a reality, the truth may be a great shock to us all. We may find kinds of life which are quite incredible and unthought of now. In this respect the writings of C. S. Lewis on space travel are particularly illuminating because they show worlds in which the ills with which we are painfully familiar have never taken root. This is a perfectly permissible imagination in conformity with Christian teaching.

When Columbus launched his expedition to discover Asia, which he called 'far Cathay', he had no idea of what he would discover, and he certainly was not looking for a vast new world, a huge continent stretching between him and his original objective. But then the public mind of his time was not filled to mental over-brimming with stories of all sorts of creatures which would be found in the lands which Columbus and his successors opened up. It happened that they found much of which they could have had no conception, and to explain which taxed their ingenuity beyond the hope of success. We on the other hand are full of thoughts and mental pictures of what lies in the great unknown of space travel. We may be completely deceived. Judging by the analogy of the past we probably are.

While the mind of man reaches forward to the distant future and the distant places involved in space travel, it has not been unmindful of the problems of this planet and its future. Ever since the last decade of the nineteenth century there have been prognostications of what lay ahead. Sometimes these were concerned, at least as far as this country, mainly with the threats to Britain from Germany, and most of these have passed into oblivion as was natural. But other prediction stories such as those of H. G. Wells – *The War of the Worlds*, *First Men in the Moon*, *The Time Machine* – still contain within themselves the hint of danger, as science expands to make them a more horrible approach to reality. I do not think that it is too much to see a genealogical connection between the sort of future depicted in the *Time Machine* and the horrors of conditioned thinking in Orwell's *1984*. Grim as this last book is, it is a question whether it is much worse than Nevile Shute's *On the Beach*. In the Shute apocalypse, no faith of any sort is left. The most significant passage in the book is perhaps that in which the Australian girl driving her car on the way to death passes a cathedral. A bell was tolling for some sort of service. That is what a modern man thought of the chances of humanity, and its future. In between the terrors which are outlined for poor little self-styled *Homo Sapiens* in these various writers, have come all sorts of other predictions. They have ranged from short-lived views as to a future in which humanity was equally divided between a Nazi and a Japanese domination; a world in which the destruction of books was the aim of government and where a society of dedicated men went about, each having in his memory a particular book, so that anyone who wanted to hear a book could go to this one man; and naturally in a feminist age there have been forecasts of a time when woman will rule man as firmly and openly as she often does subtly and hiddenly at present. I can recollect only one writer who has given any hope in his vision of the coming world. He was Robert Hugh Benson, who early in this century, in its first decade in fact, wrote two novels, entitled respectively, *The Dawn of All* and *Lord of the World*. Benson was a Catholic priest, a convert to Catholicism from the Anglican Church (he was the son of an Archbishop of Canterbury), and in these two books he delineated what he thought would be the future of the human race in the event of either a rediscovery or return to Catholicism, or the triumph of secular thought. Being a convert to the Roman Church he was perhaps too inclined to lean towards the authority of the Church. At any rate his book, *The Dawn of All*, was cordially disliked by many

Catholics as showing a future in which there would be too much sacerdotal rule. As one Irish Catholic expressed it to me, 'a horrible idea, priests with a finger in every pie'. But in his second work, *The Lord of the World*, Benson came much nearer to the mark. In this book, he deals with some period which may be thought to be about the beginning of the twenty-first century. The world has become much more unified than it is now, and far more than it was in Benson's day. There is an Eastern and a Western bloc, as at present. These two are on the verge of war, after a very long spell of peace. The world trembles on the brink of a warfare of which it has no experience and of which it can only conjecture the most horrible happenings. Meanwhile, it is a world in which religion plays an increasingly poorer part. Protestantism has gone, and Roman Catholicism stands as the main exponent in the world of a supernatural religion. But secular thought progresses from strength to strength.

Then comes a curious happening which is hailed by the majority of people as a climax, but which is in the author's intention only a beginning. This is the pacification of East and West by a great unknown personality, a man who appears from nowhere, and becomes the hope of humanity. To deal briefly with the story, this man is, in fact, anti-Christ, actually receives worship and is regarded as a kind of representative of deified humanity. Not unnaturally a fierce attack develops upon Christianity and, finally, after Rome has been bombed into rubble and most of the College of Cardinals destroyed, the last Pope is left to direct the affairs of the Church from Nazareth. The end of the story comes quite simply with the assault of the world's legions upon the remnant of the Church there, and the Second Coming of Christ. The book ends with the words: 'Then this world passed and the glory of it'.

I have left this forecast of the future for the last because I feel that it contains the greatest amount of truth. Nothing is more noticeable in the literature of the twentieth century than the disillusion which has attended some of the more optimistic of the humanists. H. G. Wells for one came in his old age to be most bitter and pessimistic about the future of mankind. His book, *Mind at the End of its Tether*, is in stark contrast to the bright visions in which he indulged earlier. Then again Earl Russell (Bertrand Russell) has not been very helpful about our fate in asking *Has Man a Future?* There being no faith in God, it is not unlikely that faith in man will also disappear. It has in most cases.

Therefore, I can foresee no abiding hope for humanity – and here we pass beyond the future only of our own country – unless we can recover our spiritual values. Many other writers speak of this, and outline various vague ways in which it can happen. But recovery of spiritual values can mean only recovery of Christianity. I am, of course, aware that there are persons who would not regard the Christian ethic as the highest of which we have any knowledge. But for most people there would I think be an agreement that Christian moral teachings are the highest, if only they could or would be put into practice. Where people make the mistake is in assuming that the ethics can be had without the creed which first accompanied them into the world. As one friend of mine put it to me, 'I've always believed in loving your enemies and forgiving injuries, but I don't want it mixed up with Athanasian Creeds'. But a tidy collection could be made out of the world's literature to show that ethics throughout the history of man have often approximated, in theory, to the teachings of the Sermon on the Mount. What is it which has given to those teachings of Christ an urgency and a practice, belated and inadequate though it may be, which no other ethic in the world can command? It has always been derived from Christian belief, and where Christian belief has faded, Christian conduct has not long continued to be substantial. It is, therefore, imperative that we recover belief in the only supernatural creed which has ever held the allegiance of highly-civilised races.

If this can be done, then the other problems in England will solve themselves. We shall recover moral earnestness and with that we shall begin to reform everything in our constitution and way of life which requires it. We shall recover a true patriotism and a true loyalty to our sovereign and to our concept of liberty. No longer can we be great in the blatantly material sense but we shall be the leaders in the march of ideas, and our material prosperity will keep step with this, because these ideas will give us a vigour of thought and action which automatically confers success in all spheres.

Is there any hope of such a revival? There is a stirring of the religious bodies which make up divided Christendom. The World Council of Churches exists and has held its greatest meeting to date in November 1961 in New Delhi. This body is made up of some 180 Churches (as the Rev. T. H. Passmore once remarked, 'Christ spoke of only one') and bodies as diverse as the Lutheran Churches and the Ortho-dox Churches of the East and of Russia and Greece are in it with the

Church of England. The Russians successfully applied for admission, and in so doing gave impressive figures of the number of Christians in Russia, even after the many years of Soviet persecution. This Council could never have been formed had there not been a very different attitude towards each other on the part of the Christians from opposed communions. Schemes for reunion are very much to the fore, and I do not think that they will all fall down. I am sure that substantial reunion will take place over the next twenty years. Already inter-communion is a fact in many cases.

At the same time, the Church of Rome which is larger than all the rest of the Christian bodies put together, is holding its Vatican Council in 1962. The main consideration of this Council is the subject of reunion. For the first time, under the benevolent rule of Pope John XXIII, Roman Catholic observers have attended the World Council of Churches, and it is possible that Protestant and Eastern Orthodox observers may attend the Vatican Council. It looks as if Bishop Gore's thought, that times of hardship may drive Christians into union, may come true quicker than we deemed feasible. Christian leaders are tending to visit Rome and to see the Pope, as in the case of the Archbishop of Canterbury (now Lord Fisher) after 400 years of mutual hostility between their communions. Even more remarkable, has been the visit to the Pope of the Moderator of the Church of Scotland. Shades of John Knox!

The world has changed so drastically and so much for the worse over the past forty years that it is easy to prophesy an ever-quickening descent to evil. Yet in a return to religion, I believe, could be England's chance yet to show other nations how to live. The criticisms I have advanced are not of matters which cannot be righted. They can still be altered for the better. While I was deeply pondering these subjects, as many others are now doing, I happened to attend the Annual United Service of the Guilds of the City of London. This is a very splendid ceremony which takes place at St Paul's Cathedral. By many it may be viewed as merely another example of the picturesque survivals which decorate British life. But on this particular occasion I believe that it served to awaken in many minds an awareness of the spiritual factor which ought to inform and influence the whole of life. The Bishop of London spoke at the service. In his remarks he said that he supposed no one in the cathedral would wish to return to the Middle Ages. There were in those centuries scenes of squalor, brutality, cruelty and extortion. Yet, he added, none of the medieval predecessors of the City magnates there present would ever have fallen into the trap of separating religion from everyday life, of regarding religion as 'a week-end cottage of the soul'. The connection of the City and its government and companies with religion was still existing: in the constitution of city and livery companies there were four strands, namely religion, charity, integrity and service.

After the service there was much conversation about these profound and wise remarks. The Bishop had reminded many of his hearers of truths which had lain deep hidden in their minds. Here was a case where a high prelate of the Church had indeed discharged his duty, with the timely word of the spirit to those in exalted places. Is it too late for the wind of the Spirit of God to breathe through this nation, making the dry bones stir and live?

I have set out what I believe to be the truth about the ramshackle British Establishment. Yet it can be reformed, and a worthwhile Establishment created from it, if all serious men and women in our country will direct their attention to that end.

Appendices

I. THE GROWTH OF THE IMPERIAL IDEA

THE first really great ruler in England after the Roman withdrawal, Offa of Mercia, was in some considerable sense the over-lord, not only of the other princes of the Heptarchy, but of the Celtic rulers in the rest of Britain. Offa was treated with respect as an equal by Charlemagne, although the latter must have been far more powerful and was the representative, as he claimed, of the old Roman Empire. Offa used the Greek title of Basileus, which among the Saxon princes was regarded as a title of great dignity and honour. He was Bretwalda, or Ruler of the Britons; so, too, was each Saxon Supremo as the States of the Heptarchy rose and fell. Athelstan was certainly so regarded after his victory at Brunanburh in 937. There is the famous incident of Edgar being rowed on the Dee by seven tributary princes. When a Danish king became the Christian sovereign of England, his adopted country was the centre of an empire, for Canute ruled Norway and Denmark in addition to England. Most important of all, William the Conqueror enforced upon the Scottish king and the Welsh princes the claims which he had inherited from his Saxon predecessors, for William claimed to be by law as well as conquest King of England. He was the Lord Paramount of Britain. Moreover, with his reign began the association of England with overseas territories which came under the same Crown. An English empire, i.e. an empire of which England is the nucleus, dates from the eleventh century. At first the Normans felt themselves the owners of England, but within three or four generations their baronial representatives were saying – *noluimus leges Angliae mutari* – 'we don't want the customs of Old England changed'. Under Henry II the English king's rule reached from Scotland to the Pyrenees. Normandy was lost under his son John in 1204, but, meanwhile, Ireland had been brought within the sphere of English rule and influence. The English still retained control of Guienne and Gascony, in fact, for three hundred years. Wales was conquered in 1284 and Scotland in 1295, being later lost. With the fourteenth century came the most astonishing effort of all at English domination. Edward III claimed in 1340 the throne of France. From this claim derived the usage of quartering the arms of England with those of France, France being the senior partner, which persisted for 460 years. On one occasion a king of England, James II, who had nothing to call his own, sought refuge with the King of France whom he had (heraldically) dethroned. Edward III's real wish, as writers like Col. Burns in England and Prof. Perroy in France have pointed out, was not to become King of France, but to secure outright possession of his western French territories. At the Treaty of Bretigny (1360) this was obtained, together with possession of Calais, whereupon Edward renounced his claim to the French throne. The claim was soon revived by his great-grandson, Henry V, who reconquered Normandy, while the baby, Henry VI, was actually crowned King of France in Notre Dame. Thanks to the inspiration of Joan of Arc, all France, save Calais, was lost by 1453. Calais itself went in 1558, but it was not more than fifty years before a new and much mightier empire came under the Crown, which could by then truly be called British. Scotland was united with England and the foundations of the Thirteen American Colonies were laid, together with possession of the sovereignty over Newfoundland. From this period, 350 years ago, the British Empire grew despite the terrible blow of the secession of the United States. Growth went on until one-quarter of the earth's surface, and one-quarter of its population was by 1914 under British rule. After the 1914-18 war the Empire was increased by the inclusion of the man-dated territories, so that Palestine, East and West Africa, and some Pacific islands came in from the vanquished countries, Turkey and Germany.

II. THE ROYAL PROCLAMATION OF 1960

'Whereas on the 9th day of April 1952, I did declare in Council My Will and pleasure that I and My Children shall be styled and known as of the House and Family of Windsor, and that My descend-ants, other than female descendants who marry and their descendants, shall bear the name of Windsor:

'And, whereas, I have given further consideration to the position of those of My descendants who will enjoy neither the style, title or attribute of Royal Highness nor the titular dignity of Prince, and for whom, therefore, a surname will be necessary.

'And, whereas, I have concluded that the Declaration made by

Me on the 9th day of April 1952, should be varied in its application to such persons:

'Now, therefore, I declare My Will and Pleasure that, while I and My children shall continue to be styled and known as the House and Family of Windsor, My descendants other than descendants enjoying the style, title or attribute of Royal Highness and the titular dignity of Prince or Princess and female descendants who marry and their descendants shall bear the name of Mountbatten-Windsor'.

The Prince Philip's family surname is Schleswig-Holstein-Sönder-borg-Glücksburg. He is by birth a member of the royal house of Greece, which is a branch of the royal family of Denmark. This fact explains why the Prince, on becoming a naturalised British subject in 1947, renounced his rights to the thrones of Greece and of Denmark. It may be of interest to trace the Duke's ancestry: He is the only son of Prince Andrew of Greece (who died in 1944), and who married Princess Alice, the elder daughter of H.S.H. Prince Louis of Batten-berg (later the 1st Marquess of Milford Haven, grandfather of the present Marquess, and father of Earl Mountbatten). Prince Philip has, or had, four elder sisters, (one was killed in an air accident in 1937). All of them have married Germans. Prince Andrew was the younger brother of Constantine I (King of Greece, and grandfather of the present king, Paul I). The father of Constantine I was George I, who in 1863 was elected King of the Hellenes, at the age of eighteen. George I was the younger brother of Frederick VIII of Denmark. Allied with the royal house of Denmark, and so with that of Greece, is the house of Holstein. One branch of this is named as: Schleswig-Holstein-Sönderborg-Augustenburg. The head of this is the Duke of Slesvig-Holstein. The second branch is that of Schleswig-Holstein-Sönderborg-Glücksburg, the head of which is a duke. The various editions of the Almanac de Gotha abound in information on the Prince Philip's paternal line.

III. THE HOUSE OF LORDS AS A COURT OF LAW

One of the most important functions of the Lords is exercised by a small body of the law lords who sit apart to try cases as a final court of appeal from England, Scotland and Northern Ireland. I have alluded to the trial of peers by their peers which was abolished in 1948, but it is very important that no one should confuse the trial of peers by their peers in the House of Lords with the sittings of the Lords in the sense of the highest court in the United Kingdom. The story of the development of that supreme court is in itself a striking commentary on the development of our institutions. With only late exceptions, the House of Lords has come to be what it is in the legal system of England without legal enactments and by the process of growth and adaptation. Originally – before and after the Norman Conquest – the King had his Great Council. This not only dealt with matters of policy, and conducted administration, but also made laws. Gradually in the course of 300 years there arose the Parliament. The Upper House, in its greatest members, had always been present in the Great Council. Now there was added the House of Commons. But long before the Model Parliament of 1295, or even that of Simon de Montfort in 1265, the Courts of Law had begun to function. Their very name derives from the presence of the sovereign whose justice they administered. Steadily the fabric of the common law was built up, with the growth of statutes. Some of the most abidingly important of the latter, such as the famous *Quia Emptores* of 1291 which lies at the basis of English land law, were passed by assemblies of the magnates without a House of Commons being in session. At the same time it was often impossible for the subject to secure justice because there was no precedent in the common law, or perhaps not even a form of action by which he could proceed. He therefore tended to appeal to the sovereign, through the latter's Chancellor, for help. In this way the Chancery jurisdiction, which has been considered in chapter nine, came into being. But also there was the final court of Parliament, and appeals came to lie to this, not only from the courts of Common law, but in addition from the Court of Chancery.

Why did appeal lie to the Lords and not to the Commons as well? 'It was held by all the judges in the reign of Henry VII that error lay from the King's Bench not to the Council but to Parliament. This meant the Council in Parliament and would apply to the Lords but not to the Commons who were not councillors. In any case the Commons had always been concerned primarily with the satisfaction of the grievances of those whom they represented and, wanted to avoid the duty of dealing with judicial matters'. (O. Hood Phillips, *The Principles of the English Law and the Constitution*, 1939, p. 458.)

It was not until 1844 that the lay peers were finally dissuaded from sitting on appeals and expressing their opinion in judgements. Possibly one reason for their persistence is that for a long time there was a great dearth of law lords in the House. About the middle of the last century, it was quite frequent for one law lord to hear and determine an appeal with a purely formal quorum of perhaps two or three peers who possessed a legal qualification which they had never employed in practice. It was to remedy this shortage of legally qualified lords that a life peerage was bestowed upon a very distinguished judge, Sir James Parke, with the title of Wensleydale, as already mentioned. It was to this common-sense attempt that the House of Lords objected when it decided that a life peerage could not allow a man to sit in the Lords.

Consequently, it is not surprising that the appellate jurisdiction of the Lords should have been lightly regarded. So much so that when great reform of English law culminated in the Supreme Court of Judicature Acts (1873-76), the appellate jurisdiction was at first abolished. This section (No. 30) of the 1873 Act never actually came into operation. In 1876 the position was righted by the Appellate Jurisdiction Act, 1876. Under this the present arrangements of the House of Lords as a law court were laid down. The Law Lords were the Lord Chancellor, the Lords of Appeal in Ordinary, i.e., life peers created under the Act, and peers who have held or hold high judicial office. It was necessary for three persons with such high qualification to be present to hear an appeal. In order for anyone to qualify for appointment as a Lord of Appeal he must have either held high judicial office for two years or have practised at the Bar for fifteen years. It became possible to have peers under this Act (and its successors) who possessed knowledge of the Scottish legal system.

There is no provision in the Acts for the exclusion of lay or otherwise unqualified peers from sitting on appeals, and, in fact, an instance of such conduct occurred in 1883. But reliance has been placed upon the good sense of lay peers and that has been sufficient without legal enactment.

This august Court is the final word on matters of law. Its decisions can be altered only by statute. It sits in an atmosphere of calm and quietude which is so profound that forensic eloquence would be completely out of place in it. Yet the judges, unlike their brethren in the lower courts, wear no formal robes. Lounge suits seem very commonplace for those who are to dispense the truths of justice undefiled.

The House of Lords retains two other kinds of legal jurisdiction. One is that of impeachment, which is a process of criminal proceedings initiated against anyone, whether peer or commoner, by the House of Commons. The other is that of the jurisdiction of the House in matters of privilege. It can punish contempts directed against it. It can through the Committee of Privileges deal with claims to peerages, provided the matter has been referred to it by the Crown.

IV. GENERAL NOTE CONCERNING OLIVER CROMWELL

The Cromwellian revolution has now been studied by writers of all shades of sympathy. Because the principles which it evokes are vital in this country, it has not become a subject for historians alone.

An excellent short life is *Oliver Cromwell* by C. V. Wedgwood (Duckworth, 1956). This is a study in the main sympathetic to Cromwell. One item of great interest lies in the remark on page 19: 'No greater mistake can be made than to assume that Cromwell belonged at this, or indeed, at any time to the land-owning plutocracy.' I think there is a misunderstanding here which needs to be corrected by a reading of such different writers as Sir Bernard Burke in *Vicissitudes of Families* or Prof. R. H. Tawney. In the various editions of the *Landed Gentry* the Cromwell lineage is given, under the name of a representative in the female line, the latest being in the family of Bush. The male line of the Cromwells, descendants of Oliver, expired in 1821 with an Oliver Cromwell, a grocer on Snow Hill, London. The Cromwells were a junior line of the rich family, to whom Miss Wedgwood refers on the same page. There is one tradition at least that Oliver's ancestors were derived from the same stock as the Lords Cromwell, whose title is still extant, and who were probably of Norman origin. Miss Wedgwood has a Bibliographical Note in which she refers to 'an exhaustive bibliography of Oliver Cromwell' compiled by Prof. Wilbur Cortez Abbott (Cambridge, Mass. 1929).

Many of the greatest writers in English literature and English historical writing have endeavoured to evaluate Cromwell. The extraordinary nature of his life whereby a private man, a small squire, overturned a kingdom and all its ancient institutions has fascinated great minds in the past 200 years. Sir Walter Scott gave what was on the whole a favourable picture of Cromwell through the medium of his novel, *Woodstock*. Thomas Carlyle devoted years of illuminating effort to the *Letters and Speeches of Oliver Cromwell*. Prof. Gardiner wrote several monumental works on the great Civil War and the Commonwealth Period. Miss Wedgwood herself has written with skill and interest on the life of Charles I. The first Lord Tweedsmuir – John Buchan – wrote a study of Cromwell, because as he expressed it, no student of the seventeenth century is satisfied until he has grappled with its greatest character.

As I have tried to show in the main text there were strong undercurrents which seemed likely to come to the surface, at the time when the abolition of episcopacy, the death of the king, and the abolition of the House of Lords, all ancient landmarks of the country, seemed to promise a complete reversal of the former order of things. Much more information to this effect can be gleaned from the writings of Maurice Ashley, such as *Financial and Commercial Policy under the Cromwellian Protectorate; or Cromwell's Generals* (Jonathan Cape, 1954). In connection with the last-named work, readers should consult a now partly forgotten historian, Henry Thomas Buckle in his *History of Civilisation in England* (The World's Classics, 1903, in 3 vols.), vol II pages 123-128. Buckle, writes at great length on what he calls 'an outbreak of a democratic spirit' in the rebellion. 'The English rebellion (was) a movement from below, an uprising from the foundations, or, as some will have it, the dregs of society'. Buckle falls into the trap of assuming that Cromwell was a brewer, because like the many other country gentlemen of the time, he brewed his own beer. On these lines, the father of the first Earl of Halifax must have been a brewer. Anyone who cares can see the impress of a seal of arms beside every signature on the death warrant of Charles I.

However, the fact remains that once the rebellion had been well and truly set in motion, it could hardly be restrained within bounds that were known. No mere parliamentary *ne plus ultra* could hold back the forces unleashed by the discovery that King, Archbishop and Lords were removable at the beck of a plain mister. While I was preparing these notes, a book was published by H. N. Brailsford, *The Levellers and the English Revolution* (Cresset Press, 1961). This book was reviewed in the *Sunday Times* (2 July 1961 by H. Trevor-Roper, under the apt heading: 'On Cromwell's Left Wing'. Cromwell put down both Levellers and Diggers and any other really democratic persons. As Hilaire Belloc remarked, nothing is more democratic than military danger shared together, and these seventeenth-century left wingers thought that having shared dangers together they should now share wealth. But the revolution which Cromwell hoped to make permanent, was to be of his own making, a strictly limited and oligarchical revolution, as it turned out. As we have seen, his reformed state would have included a monarchy, lords of a sort and a limited franchise. It would have had an efficient military and naval force, with an urge towards empire and a strong foreign policy. There was a reforming policy at home to remove many age-old anomalies and injustices. But a full-blooded democracy no more appealed to Cromwell than it did to the Whig leaders at the Glorious Revolution of 1688. As Sir Winston Churchill has said in his history, neither Charles I nor his executioner Cromwell cared for Parliaments, and both of them either tried to dismiss them, or actually did so.

In the event, Cromwell's policy failed as much as that of his opponents. It was felt throughout England that he had gone too far. This is exactly the feeling which remains in this country still whenever Cromwell's name is mentioned, except for the minority of admirers who belong to the Cromwell Association, and to the writers who have studied Cromwell's character, almost all of whom profess an admiration for him of varying degrees of fervour.

The revulsion of feeling against Cromwell attached itself to almost the whole of his administration. How efficient that administration was can be judged from a work like Mrs D. L. Hobman's *Cromwell's Master Spy:* A study of John Thurlow (Chapman and Hall, 1961). When the Cromwellian revolution was completed, the English people had their chance of a new start, and they rejected it. The price which they paid was to pass more than a century and a half with the impulse of reform, as it were, in suspense.

Readers of Butler's poem, *Hudibras*, will remember the list of people of somewhat lowly occupations who went out on revolution. Prof. Sir Walter Raleigh remarked of this catalogue: What was Milton doing in such company? Yet all were bent on reforms.

V. LORD SNOWDON AND THE N.U.J.

Soon after Lord Snowdon joined the *Sunday Times* he took a further ultra democratic step – he joined the National Union of Journalists. On this I think the best comment I can make is in the words of the

Institute of Journalists, which is the royal charter body, the charter having been bestowed by Queen Victoria, whereas the N.U.J. is purely and simply a trade union. In the April of 1962 issue of the *Journal*, the organ of the Institute of Journalists occurs the following passage (a statement by the Emergency Committee of the Council of the Institute). 'The announcement that Lord Snowdon has become a member of the National Union of Journalists, a body affiliated with the Trades Union Congress which as shown during the printing dispute of 1959, is committed to strike action and whose avowed aim is to enforce the closed shop in respect of all editorial staffs, must cause serious misgivings to many responsible journalists.

'Lord Snowdon himself may not be aware either of the political implications of his action or of the fact that the organisation he has joined has proscribed journalists who have chosen to remain outside its membership to such an extent that they have been prevented from pursuing their professional activities and earning their livelihood.

'He may also be unaware of the N.U.J. declaration that "the closed shop is not an end in itself but a means to an end and the end is that we should get a degree of control over the office." It is a matter of profound regret to the Institute of Journalists, the senior society of the profession, that Lord Snowdon should have accepted an association which might be misinterpreted and, in certain circumstances, place him in an embarrassing position in the eyes of the public.'

Perhaps the Institute of Journalists is wrong after all, in its concern for the dignity of the profession of journalism. If Lord Snowdon should become Father of the Chapel at the *Sunday Times*, would this not be advantageous to journalists?

In the meanwhile I learn from *The Times* (21 May 1962) that the Snowdon Mountain Railway has offered to Lord Snowdon and his heirs in perpetuity free travel up and down the mountain, which offer has been accepted.

Index

185